PRINCIPLES OF NATURE

"Deism also declares that the practice of a pure, natural, and uncorrupted virtue is the essential duty, and constitutes the highest dignity, of man; that the powers of man are competent to all the great purposes of human existence; that science, virtue, and happiness are the great objects that ought to awake the mental energies and draw forth the moral affections of the human race."

BY ELIHU PALMER

With an introduction by Bob Johnson

D1160804

Other books from the World Union of Deists:

The Age of Reason, The Complete Edition;
Reason: The Only Oracle of Man;
God Gave Us Reason, Not Religion;
Deism: A Revolution in Religion, A Revolution in You;
An Answer to C.S. Lewis' Mere Christianity

CONTENTS

"*Truth ought to be the object of every person; for without truth there can be no real happiness to a thoughtful mind, or any assurance of happiness hereafter. It is the duty of man to obtain all the knowledge he can, and then make the best use of it.*"

—Thomas Paine

INTRODUCTION

Elihu Palmer was an American freethinker who was greatly inspired by one of America's greatest Founding Fathers, Thomas Paine. Like Paine, Palmer was an uncompromising and happy Deist.

Born in 1764 in Canterbury, Connecticut, Palmer was too young to take part in the American Revolution as Paine had done. However, the same free, limitless and inquiring spirit that was in Paine and the other revolutionaries was also in Elihu Palmer.

His free spirit showed itself after he graduated from Dartmouth in 1787, shortly after accepting a position as a Presbyterian minister. At that time Elihu Palmer evolved into a Deist. As a Deist he could no longer, with a clear conscience, promote Christianity since he believed in God based on the application of his reason on the designs found in Nature. As a Deist Palmer saw that these designs in Nature point to a Designer of Nature. Also as a Deist, Palmer's reason would not allow him to accept unreasonable claims made in the Bible and promoted by Christianity. He was honest enough to realize this

and courageous enough to end his career as a Christian cler-
gyman which he had spent years studying for and, from that
point forward, spent all of his time and life promoting Deism.

1796 was the year that Palmer started the first ever Deist
organization in the United States, the Deistical Society. He
founded the organization in New York City and in 1800 he
started the Deist publication, *The Temple of Reason*. In 1803 he
founded another Deist publication, *View of the Moral World*.
Even though he lost his vision due to yellow fever in 1793, he
never stopped writing for Deism and promoting Deism every
way he could. Both of his wives (in 1793 his first wife died
from yellow fever) were indispensable assets to him in the
promotion of Deism. They both took Deism to heart and even
after his death in 1806 his second wife remained a staunch
Deist helping their mutual good friend, Thomas Paine as he
continued the fight to free people from the fear and superstition of the "revealed" religions through the natural religion/
philosophy of Deism.

In 1801 Elihu Palmer published the book you're now holding in your hands, *Principles of Nature; or a Development of the
Moral Causes of Happiness and Misery among the Human Species*. We've decided to keep this book in its original form and
style without updating the language in order not to deviate
from Elihu Palmer's original ideas and thoughts.

Like Thomas Paine's *The Age of Reason* and Ethan Allen's
and Thomas Young's *Reason: The Only Oracle of Man*, *Principles of Nature* is a hard hitting, thought provoking Deistic
work which removes the superstition from belief in God. By

so doing, it also brings to light the fact that there is no need for the clergy.

Like the other Deist writers before him, Palmer did not pull any punches! For example, he referred to Jesus as an "illegitimate Jew." His concern was not if he offended people, it was to tell the truth. Palmer obviously saw the truth of Thomas Paine's statement, "Such is the irresistible nature of truth that all it asks, and all it wants, is the liberty of appearing."

Palmer's open and frank character and style was greatly appreciated by Thomas Paine. After receiving a copy of *Principles of Nature*, Paine wrote to Palmer, "I received, by Mr. Livingston, the letter you wrote to me, and the excellent work [the *Principles of Nature*] you have published. I see you have thought deeply on the subject, and expressed your thoughts in a strong and clear style. The hinting and intimating manner of writing that was formerly used on subjects of this kind, produced skepticism, but not conviction. It is necessary to be bold. Some people can be reasoned into sense, and others must be shocked into it. Say a bold thing that will stagger them, and they will begin to think."

Due to the unrelenting and concerted effort of the "revealed" religions, Christianity in particular, Deism has been ignored by the history writers. Considering America's historic connection with Deism through its Founding Fathers such as Thomas Paine, Benjamin Franklin, George Washington, Thomas Jefferson and other key founders, not to mention the Declaration of Independence, which is a Deistic document in that it mentions God only in Deistic terms and never in Biblical terms, Deism rightfully belongs in the forefront of every American's mind. Looking at reality, if America's Founding Fathers were sincere Christians, the American Revolution never would have happened. They would have been prohibited from opposing the established government/powers that be based on Romans 13:1-2 which reads, "Let every soul be subject unto the higher powers. For there is no power but of God: the powers that be are ordained of God. Whosoever therefore resisteth the power, resisteth the ordinance of God: and they that resist shall receive to themselves damnation." Based on this Bible teaching, America's Founding Fathers and all who took part on behalf of the American Revolution are receiving "to themselves damnation" and are now burning in hell.

A recent religious survey, the American Religious Identification Survey 2008, shows there are millions of people in the U.S. who are Deists but don't know it. The World Union of Deists, following in the footsteps of great Deists like Thomas Paine and Elihu Palmer and both of his wives, are striving to make Deism a household word so these millions of people will realize they are **NOT** alone and that they share a great religious philosophy and identity in Deism, while at the same time letting millions of other people in the U.S. and around the world know that they have a reasonable and natural alternative to both "revealed" religions and to Atheism in Deism.

Bob Johnson
Founder and Director World Union of Deists
July 4, 2009

I'll not be made a soft and dull ey'd fool,
To shake the head, relent and sigh and yield
To Christian intercessors....
— Shakespeare, *The Merchant of Venice*

Prove all things. — I Thess. v. 21

PREFACE

God, to remove his ways from human sense,
Plac'd Heaven from earth so far, that earthly sight,
If it presume, might err in things too high,
And no advantage gain.

— Milton

The establishment of theological systems, claiming divine origin, has been among the most destructive causes by which the life of man has been afflicted. History furnishes an awful picture of the sad and fatal effects of fanaticism among the nations of the earth; but history furnishes only the exterior; there is a deeper internal wound, which superstition has inflicted in the bosom of society, subversive of all moral sympathy and the fairest traits in the character of man. The sincerity with which many upright minds are attached to the Christian religion, can form no substantial objection against an unqualified investigation into its truth or falsehood. If it be founded in truth, it will stand the test of every examination—it will stand the test of all future ages, and become immortal. It is a point of justice to observe, that this work has been written under the misfortune and embarrassment of a total loss of sight. This, in the estimation of candid minds, will form at least a partial apology for verbal incorrectness, or the want of better arrangement in the construction of sentences; but it is not offered as constituting any kind of apology for errors of opinion or principle. On this head the fullest examination is invited; and, if any one can point out in what respect the principles herein advanced are inconsistent and erroneous, the author will be among the first to reject and condemn them. But this must be done upon the ground of evidence, and not of authority, as the latter bears no relation to truth. The great moral and political questions which now agitate the world, cannot be settled by an appeal to the authority of law books, theological books, or the decisions of ecclesiastical councils; they rest upon the broad basis of evidence, and by this principle alone they must be determined. The circumstance that the author was once a public speaker in the cause of Christianity, which is here opposed, so far from forming a reasonable objection against the perusal of this work, ought to become an additional motive of attention; for it was by a candid and attentive investigation into the character of revealed religion, that he became convinced that it was neither true nor divine. It was, therefore, a duty which he owed to the integrity of his own mind, and what was deemed the best interests of human society, to abandon that system, and assume a higher and better ground—that of Nature, and the immutability of her laws. If any one should be disposed to censure on this account, let him remember that there is more honor and much more utility in the relinquishment than in the retention of errors. The new chapters contained in this edition are intended to awaken a spirit of philosophic inquiry in every description of adherents to the ancient regimen, and to induce them to pass once more in review the religious theories to which they have been so strongly attached. The principal design of the author, through the whole of this work, has been to give to moral principle a basis as durable as time, and as immortal as the specific succession of human existence; and to render the sentiment of virtue, as far as possible, independent of all the theological reveries of antiquity.

CHAPTER I

The Power of Intellect, its Duty, and the Obstacles that Oppose its Progress

The sources of hope and consolation to the human race are to be sought for in the energy of intellectual powers. To these, every specific amelioration must bear a constant and invariable reference; and whatever opposes the progress of such a power, is unquestionably in most pointed opposition to the best and most important interests of our species. The organic construction of man induces a strong conclusion that no limits can possibly be assigned to his moral and scientific improvements. The question relative to the nature and substance of the human mind, is of much less consequence than that which relates to the extent of force and capacity, and the diversified modes of beneficial application. The strength of human understanding is incalculable, its keenness of discernment would ultimately penetrate into every part of nature, were it permitted to operate with uncontrolled and unqualified freedom. It is because this sublime principle of man has been constantly the object of the most scurrilous abuse, and the most detestable invective from superstition,

that his moral existence has been buried in the gulf of ignorance, and his intellectual powers tarnished by the ferocious and impure hand of fanaticism. Although we are made
capable of sublime reflections, it has hitherto been deemed a
crime to think, and a still greater crime to speak our thoughts
after they have been conceived. The despotism of the universe had waged war against the power of the human understanding, and for many ages successfully combated its efforts,
but the natural energy of this immortal property of human
existence was incapable of being controlled by such extraneous and degrading restraints. It burst the walls of its prison,
explored the earth, discovered the properties of its component parts, analyzed their natures, and gave to them specific
classification and arrangement. Not content with terrestrial
researches, intellect abandoned the earth, and traveled in
quest of science through the celestial regions. The heavens
were explored, the stars were counted, and the revolutions
of the planets subjected to mathematical calculation. All
nature became the theater of human action, and man in his
unbounded and ardent desire attempted to embrace the universe. Such was the nature of his powers, such their strength
and fervor, that hopes and anticipations were unqualified
and unlimited. The subordinate objects in the great mass of
existence were decompounded, and the essential peculiarities of their different natures delineated with astonishing
accuracy and wonderful precision. Situated in the midst of a
world of physical wonders, and having made some progress
in the analytical decomposition of material substances, and
the relative position of revolving orbs, man began to turn
his powers to the nice disquisitions of the subtle properties
of his mental existence. Here the force of his faculties was
opposed by the darkness and difficulties of the subject; and

superstition, ever ready to arrest and destroy moral improvement, cast innumerable difficulties in the way, and the bewildered mind found this part of the system of nature less accessible than the physical universe, whose prominent disparities struck the understanding and presented clear discrimination. The ignorance and barbarism of former ages, it is said, furnish an awful intimation of the imbecility of our mental powers, and the hopeless condition of the human race. If thought be reflected back for the purpose of recognizing through a long night of time, the miseries and ignorance of the species, there will be found, no doubt, powerful causes of lamentation; but courage will be resuscitated when the energy of intellect is displayed, and the improvement of the world, which has been already made, shall be clearly exhibited to view. It is not sufficient that man acknowledge the possession of his intellectual powers, it is also necessary that these powers should be developed, and their force directed to the discovery of direct principle, and the useful application of it to social life; errors, evils, and vices, every where exist, and by these the world has been rendered continually wretched, and the history of mankind furnishes the dreadful lessons, and shocks the sensibility of every human being. The savage ferocity of despotism has destroyed the harmony of society; the unrelenting cruelty of superstition has cut asunder the finest fibers that ever concreted the hearts of intelligent beings. It has buried beneath its gloomy vale all the moral properties of our existence, and entombed in the grave of ignorance and terror, the most sublime energies, and the purest affections of the human mind. An important duty is therefore imposed upon intellect, and a departure from its faithful performance should be ranked among the crimes which have most disgraced and injured the felicity of the world. If the few philanthropists who have embarked in the cause of humanity, have not been adequately rewarded, it is, nevertheless, true, that the principle and force of duty remain the same, unbroken and incapable of being abrogated. It is the discovery and propagation of truth which ought to engage the attention of man, and call forth the powerful activity of his mind.

The nature of ancient institutions, instead of forming a reason against the activity of mind, should be considered as constituting a double stimulus; these institutions are such a complete abandonment of every just and correct principle; they have been so destructive in their operation and effects, that nothing but the strong and energetic movement of the human understanding will be capable of subverting them. The whole earth has been made the wretched abode of ignorance and misery; and to priests and tyrants these dreadful effects are to be attributed. These are the privileged monsters who have subjugated the earth, destroyed the peace and industry of society, and committed the most atrocious of all robberies; that which had robbed human nature of its intellectual property, leaving all in a state of waste and barrenness. Moses, Zoroaster, Jesus, and Mahomet, are names celebrated in history; but what are they celebrated for? Have their institutions softened the savage ferocity of man? Have they developed a clear system of principle, either moral, scientific, or philosophical? Have they encouraged the free and unqualified operation of intellect, or, rather, by their institutions, has not a gloom been thrown over the clearest subjects, and their examination prohibited under the severest penalties? The successors and followers of these men have adhered to the destructive lessons of their masters with undeviating tenacity. This has formed one of the most powerful obstacles to the progress of improvement, and still threatens, with eternal "damnation," that man who shall call in question the truth of their "dogmas," or the divinity of their systems.

The political tyranny of the earth coalesced with this phalanx of religious despots, and the love of science and of virtue was nearly banished from the world. Twelve centuries of moral and political darkness, in which Europe was involved, had nearly completed the destruction of human dignity, and every thing valuable or ornamental in the character of man. During this long and doleful night of ignorance, slavery, and superstition, Christianity reigned triumphant; its doctrines and divinity were not called in question. The power of the Pope, the clergy, and the church, were omnipotent; nothing could restrain their frenzy, nothing could control the cruelty of their fanaticism; with mad enthusiasm they set on foot the most bloody and terrific crusades, the object of which was to recover from infidels the "Holy Land." Seven hundred thousand men are said to have perished in the two first expeditions, which had been thus commenced and carried on by the pious zeal of the Christian church, and in the total amount, several millions were found numbered with the dead: the awful effects of religious fanaticism presuming upon the aid of heaven. It was then that man lost all his dignity, and sunk to the condition of a brute; it was then that intellect received a deadly blow, from which it did not recover till the fifteenth century. From that time to the present, the progress of knowledge has been constantly accelerated; independence of mind has been asserted, and opposing obstacles have been gradually diminished. The church has resigned a part of her power, the better to retain the remainder; civil tyranny has been shaken to its center in both hemispheres; the malignity of superstition is abating, and every species of "quackery," imposture, and imposition, are yielding to the light and power of science. An awful contest has commenced, which must terminate in the destruction of thrones and civil despotism; in the annihilation of ecclesiastical pride and domination; or, on the other hand, intellect, science, and manly virtue, will be crushed in one general ruin, and the world will retrograde towards a state of ignorance, barbarism, and misery. The latter however is an event rendered almost impossible by the discovery of the art of printing, by the expansion of mind, and the general augmentation of knowledge. Church and State may unite to form an insurmountable barrier against the extension of thought, the moral progress of nations and the felicity of nature; but let it be recollected, that the guarantee for the moral and political emancipation is already deposited in the archives of every school and college, and in the mind of every cultivated and enlightened man of all countries. It will henceforth be a vain and fruitless attempt to reduce the earth to that state of slavery of which the history of former ages has furnished such an awful picture. The crimes of ecclesiastical despots are still corroding upon the very vitals of human society; the severities of civil power will never be forgotten. The destructive influence of ancient institutions will teach us to seek in nature and the knowledge of her laws, for the discovery of those principles whose operation alone can emancipate the world from dreadful bondage. If in the succeeding chapters we shall be able to destroy any considerable portion of human errors, and establish some solid truths, our labours will bear a relation to the progressive improvement of the human race, which, to intelligent minds, is of all considerations the most beneficial and important.

CHAPTER II

Theology and its Effects

The impressions that are made on the human mind by the awful and tremendous powers of nature, have filled it with terror and astonishment. If by a laborious investigation of the universe, and the laws by which it is regulated; if by an examination of our own constitution and the refined properties of our existence; if from a view of the moral and physical world, in the aggregate, we are led to the idea of simple Theism including all possible perfection; it will nevertheless be found substantially true, that with all savage nations, and even with the mass of the people in civilized countries, that no such sublime conception has ever formed any part of their systems of theology. Rude, immoral, and incoherent opinions have been heaped together upon this subject, and gods innumerable have been fabricated by a distempered and disordered imagination. It is only with those who have made some progress in science, that any clear and correct ideas of theology have been found; the God of Ignorance has always been an immortal monster, whose attributes spread terror through the whole animal world. The power of thought, directed to the examination

7

of the laws of nature, or to the science of ontology, is pressed by an ultimate necessity to the admission of an immortal principle, to the faint conception of an eternal Being, whose perfections guarantee the existence and harmony of the universe. The essence of such a Being is inconceivable, and that mind which has no doubt on the reality of the case, is, nevertheless, incompetent to the discovery of mode, manner, or place of residence. If the material world be excluded from constituting any share in the essence of such a Being, the refinements and speculations will afterwords become extremely subtle, and conception will, perhaps, be nearly lost in the spirituality of the subject. The principle of causation is, of all others, the most difficult of examination, because it includes the idea of an infinite series in which the last point at which the mind arrives presents a new difficulty not less than the former, and involving the idea of eternal progression. Metaphysical reasoning on the subject is, however, reserved to occupy a place near the close of this Work, where Theism and its combatants will receive a suitable share of reflection. At present it is sufficient that we refer the universe, its laws, and order, to the divinity of thought emanating from the most perfect of all beings. It has been a great question, how far the principle of theology affects the principle and practice of virtue. It can be matter of no doubt, in the first place, that a corrupt and vitiated theology has ever been the bane of morality, and produced effects of the most destructive and detestable nature. An infinite Being, clothed with immoral attributes, and yet made an object of worship and affection, will indubitably pervert the finest sensations of the human heart, and render savage and ferocious the character of man. This is not conjecture, it is verified by facts; the history of all churches proves it beyond contradiction. It is natural to expect such an effect; the Being that is worshiped is presented as a pattern, and to imitate his properties is declared to be an essential duty. If such a Being commit murder, or at any time gives orders to the human race to perform such a cruel act, the order once given is the signal for military assassination, national vengeance, or the exercise of domestic resentment. The world becomes a field of blood, and man is slaughtered in the name of Heaven. From the introduction of Christianity into the world to the present moment, there is scarcely a single war that has taken place in Europe but what has verified this opinion. The church has always been in danger, it is in danger still, and always will be, so long as there shall be found on earth a single privileged impostor, to sound in the name of Heaven, the trumpet of alarm among the nations of the world. The purest ideas of the Divinity are necessary for the correct operation of the moral powers of man; there cannot remain a shadow of doubt, when recourse is made to the history of the Jews and Christians, that the god or gods whom they have adored have produced an unfavorable effect upon their moral temperament and habits. The Jewish god is denominated a god of vengeance, wrath, and fury. He gives commands for the indiscriminate massacre of men, women, and children, declaring that not a soul should be left alive. The God of the Jews is inherited by the Christians with additional specimens of injustice and immorality. An infinite and eternal Son, equal to himself, becomes the object of his wrath, and on him with unrelenting severity he wreaks his terrible vengeance. This awful and immoral action is considered in the view of the Christian believer, as an excellent preparatory step to the exercise of gratitude, and the overflowings of filial affections. When man makes to himself gods of such a character, it were far better that he had been destitute of all theological opinions, or that his adoration should have been offered to that resplendent luminary that enlightens the world, and vivifies the productions of the earth. The principle of morality is founded in the nature of man, and modified by his reciprocal relations; this principle cannot be augmented in its force or application by a reference to those barbarous phantoms and incongruous beings which the theology of the Jews and Christians, as well as all savage nations, has presented to view. Individuals and nations will always be wicked so long as they adore a divinity of loose and immoral character. Theology must first be rendered pure, and then it will become a question of magnitude, what influential relation it bears to the science of morality and happiness of the world.

CHAPTER III

Christian Theology

Believers in the Christian system of religion are seldom aware of the difficulties into which their theological theories have plunged them. They are in habits of bestowing on this religion the most unqualified applause, and in most cases, no doubt, the most sincere approbation; but the errors and absurdities, the immorality and the incorrectness of principle, have never made any serious impression upon their minds. The dreadful idea of opposing that which has been called divine, strikes with terror the uninstructed mind, and ignorance feeds the ecclesiastical deception. Ignorance is an excellent friend to an ancient system of error, to the church and the different projects by which mankind have been enslaved. If you can once persuade a man that he is totally ignorant of the subject on which you are about to discourse, you can make him believe any thing. Impositions of this kind are furnished by every day's experience; and the victim of such imposition is commonly the first to applaud the instrument of his ruin.

Nothing can be more true, nothing more certain, or important, than that a man owes to himself due respect, that his intellect is an object of veneration, and its result interwoven with the best interests of human society. The distorted exhibitions of imaginary beings contained in all ancient theology ought to excite within us a strong desire to discover truth, and reclaim the dignity which nature gave to man. Fanaticism, when armed with the artillery of Heaven, ought not to be permitted to shake the throne or empire of reason; the base is immortal, and the superstructure will be augmented in beauty and excellence, in proportion to the progress of knowledge and the destruction of religious bigotry. It is remarkable, that with many honest minds the consciousness of intellectual independence has never been realized, and fear has prevented the activity of thought and the development of truth. Names have assumed a weight and authority, which in reality does not belong to them. The church and its maxims have been revered; subordinate agents of the Creator have produced universal trepidation; the Devil has broke into the felicity of the moral world, and God himself, even with the Christian church, is an object of terror and dismay. These subjects carry along with them the most dreadful alarm, and man, amidst the reveries of supernatural theology, becomes either feeble or foolish, his power relaxed, his energy is gone, and he sinks beneath the system of fear, which it is the office of cultivated reason alone to destroy. Such are the fatal effects of all theology, but more particularly of that which is denominated Christian. The Christian world worships three infinite Gods, and one omniscient and omnipresent Devil.[1] This last being is

---

[1]These assertions have been objected to as incorrect by some believers who read the first edition of this work. The explanatory and qualifying remarks which follow this phrase in the text, ought to have silenced objections of this kind; but there are other

an object rather of terror and frightful apprehension, than of worship and adoration; but as he is clothed with nearly all of the attributes which this system of religion has ascribed to its divinity, or divinities, and as the latter is also clothed with the awful qualities of wrath and vengeance, it would be difficult to offer any good reason why the one should be entitled, in the view of the Christian believer, to more homage than the other, since between them there is so striking a resemblance of character. But whether Christian theology represents the Devil as an object of worship or only of fear, it is nevertheless certain, that he is a very important and essential character in the drama therein acted. He holds a prominent and conspicuous place in this wonderful system of mythology, and his destruction would go far to the ruin of the scheme itself. There are many other subordinate agents, who are actors in the

---

Scriptural considerations which will abundantly destroy the force of the objection. God is represented as a being of wrath, vengeance, and fury—so also is the Devil! The worship of God consists in a very high degree in the sentiment of fear. The fear of the Lord is the beginning of wisdom, fear God and keep his commandments, &c. Christian believers are also most terribly afraid of the Devil; if the sentiment of fear be worship in the one case, why should it not be so considered in the other case? But this is not all; the description given of these two beings in Holy Writ, is so perfectly similar, that believers, in order to be consistent, ought to include them both as objects of worship. Speaking of God, the Scriptures say, "He was unto me as a Bear lying in wait, and as a Lion in secret places." Lam. iii. 10. And of the Devil, "He goeth about like a roaring Lion, seeking whom he may devour." I Peter v. 8. The only distinction here is, that the one was a roaring lion, and the other did not roar; but this deficiency is made up by coupling with the still lion, and a still bear also; for these two put together would probably be about equal, in point of terror, to the roaring lion. When Christian believers are so inconsistent as to worship these immoral monsters, or either of them, they ought to cease to charge others with lies and blasphemies. As to the first part of the phrase, That the Christian world worships three infinite Gods—this is "certainly" true, and demonstrated by the single consideration, that they attribute infinite perfection to each person in the Trinity. The unintelligible union of these three persons cannot destroy in any degree whatever, the infinite perfection ascribed to each; it therefore remains true, that the Christian world really worship three infinite Gods, or infinite persons, which is exactly the same thing.

Christian scenes, such as angels, ghosts, and witches; these, however, are not considered as objects of adoration, but are only to be treated with that degree of civility and respect, to which their station in this celestial and mythological aristocracy may justly entitle them. This variegated groups of gods, devils, angels, ghosts, and witches, is what constitutes essentially the supernatural theology, or rather mythology of the Christian world. One sect, the most ancient, and like all others, in their own estimation, the most orthodox, have added one female divinity to complete the beauty and wonder of the scheme. The "Virgin Mary," among the Papists, is called the mother of God; and having produced so respectable an offspring, is frequently addressed with prayers and supplications, and to her, also, divine honors are paid.

Next to the absurdity of the leading idea contained in the nature of this theological system, is that branch of it which violates all the rules of arithmetical calculation, and mathematical proportion; that which violates all ideas of common sense and common understanding, the awful doctrine of the Trinity. "The Father is God, the Son is God, and the Holy Ghost is God; and yet there are not Three Gods, but One God. The Father is Almighty, the Son is Almighty, and the Holy Ghost is Almighty; yet there are not three Almighties, but one Almighty."(1) The essence of this doctrine is, that there is but one infinite and perfect being, yet there are three infinite and perfect beings. When the Christian is asked how many Gods there are, he will answer, there is but one. If the inquiry be made, how many persons this God is divided into, the answer is three; but to each of these three persons all possible perfection is attributed, and yet in a compound state, the whole mass of perfection continues the same. Let this doctrine be subjected to rational investigation, and its absurdity and contradiction must strike with astonishment every correct mind. There cannot possibly exist in nature more than one infinite, eternal, and perfect being; one infinity swallows up all others, and it is impossible to add to that which is already as great as it can be. If God the Father possess all possible excellence, if he be infinite in extent, infinite in duration, there can be no space or time in which any other infinite being could possibly exist. Two infinities must either coincide and coalesce, and then they would become one, or they would destroy each other. If the Father is possessed of infinite wisdom, such attribute cannot belong either to the Son, or to the Holy Ghost; if the Son, the second person, possessed such infinite wisdom, it would operate as a disfranchisement of the other two; the same will apply to the "Holy Ghost," in exclusion of his competitors; there can be but one infinite; a double infinite is a double absurdity, and the Trinitarian idea in incongruous and impossible. If the assertion be made, that one is equal to three, and that three are no more than one, all numerical distinction is totally destroyed, and man consents to become a fool upon the plainest points. Trinitarian declarations are direct contradictions to each other; the part is as great as the whole, and the whole is no greater than the part; three infinities put together make only one, and the destruction of two of them does not diminish the mass of existence or perfection. If facts did not stare us in the face, we should never have believed that it was in the power of superstition to have perverted in so gross a manner the human understanding. In all the common concerns and calculations of human life, Christians themselves, practically declare, that they do not believe in the doctrine of the Trinity. In these concerns, they would be very unwilling that a part should be considered as equal to the whole, or that the whole should be estimated no higher than the part; they would not consent to destroy all numerical distinction, nor would they be willing to annihilate the just ideas of discrimination, by which their interest is supported; but although in common life they would reject all this, yet in theology the nature of things is stripped of its true character, and every species of just distinction is perverted or destroyed. This doctrine of the Trinity, Christianity has borrowed from the ancient heathen ideas, and the church has incorporated it for the purposes of mystery and ecclesiastical imposition. It was found among the reveries of Plato, and being transferred to the followers of Jesus, it has appeared under the modification, and with the names of Father, Son, and Holy Ghost. Thus modified, it became the foundation of a cruel and ferocious dogma, that eternal damnation should be the portion of him who called in question this holy mystery. The spirit of this trinitarian opinion has diffused itself through several other parts of the Christian system, and the idea of an atonement is not the least shocking amongst the consequences that are to be ascribed to this theological absurdity. The followers of the Son of Mary boast of the purity of their theistical doctrine; but a candid examination of it proves, that it is nothing more than a modification of the mythological opinions of all ancient and barbarous nations. [1. See St. Athanasius's Creed.]

CHAPTER IV

The Bible, or the Sacred Writings of the Jews and Christians

Among all nations that have pretended to any kind of literary improvement, there have always been found ambitious, designing, and fanatic men, who are impelled by one or the other of these considerations to become leaders of influential characters among the beings who surround them. Superiority of talents or improvements, constituted a ground of hope and strong belief, that they should succeed in an attempt of this kind. Advantage was taken of human ignorance, and the most destructive and erroneous plans were introduced and established by length of time and the force of authority. In nations not at all, or very little improved, tradition has supplied the place of sacred writings, and they have been equally the dupes of those unprincipled chieftains who have assumed authority over them. Moses and Mahomet governed their followers with a rod of iron, and a military despotism. They were savage and ferocious men, crafty and intriguing, and they knew how to subject to their will the stupid but unfortunate followers who

17

were devoted to their views. If Jesus was more mild, benevolent, and temperate, it was because he had less power, and because his disposition was less cruel and resentful. His followers, when clothed with power, have not paid a very high compliment to their master, for the history of their conduct evinces the most malignant design, and the earth has been drenched in blood, to defend that system of religion, of which the meek and lowly Jesus is reputed to be the author.

The Christian religion is a compound and combination of all the theological writings of the followers of Moses and Jesus. We have no evidence that either of these men wrote any part, either of the Old or New Testament. From Genesis to the Apocalypse of St. John, a vast variety of fact, fable, principle, wickedness, and error is exhibited to view. The book, though bound together, appears to be in many respects discordant; the historical part has no accurate connection; the moral part is distorted, deficient, or wicked; the doctrinal parts are either unintelligible, or contrary to moral and philosophical truth. These positions shall be proved in the course of the examination of these sacred writings; it is sufficient for the present that the consideration which relates to the origin and nature of such productions, should form the basis of our inquiry. It is because man has forgotten the dignity of his nature; it is because he does not realize the force of his faculties, that he consents to yield to the impositions of superstition. What is a book, whether it be denominated sacred or not, unless the human mind is capable of discovering the evidence by which the truth of such book can be substantiated? The Bible, which means nothing more than a book; the scriptures of the Old and New Testaments, which means nothing more than the heterogeneous writings contained in the former, and the incoherent and unintelligible will of various beings contained in the latter; what are all these to the correct decisions of human intellect, unless the matter therein contained can be collated with the immortal principles of truth in the system of nature?

The title page of the Bible subjects it to a strong suspicion of fraud and deception, of error, alteration, and absurdity. It is as follows, and ought to be examined: "The Holy Bible, containing the Old and New Testaments, translated out of the original tongues, and with the former translations, diligently compared and revised, by his Majesty's special command. Appointed to be read in churches." The title page of this book, which for many centuries has been the rule of faith and action in the Christian world, is of itself sufficient to destroy its supernatural origin and divine authority. It is to be observed, that the book in the first place was denominated holy; but its holiness and divinity are both destroyed before we get through the title page. It is a well known fact, that this book was not written at first in the English language, but in Hebrew, Greek, and Latin; that it has been translated out of these languages into English; and the believer who understands no language but English, rests his faith upon the knowledge and integrity of the translators alone. He cannot tell whether these men were either scientific or honest, and consequently he does not know whether he believes what was really contained in the original writings or not. He cannot determine whether the sentiments which have drawn forth the affections of his heart, have really emanated from God, or proceeded from the mind of man; he cannot tell whether the supposed truths of the gospel are the result of human or divine power. If the sentiments and the doctrines be consistent with the nature of things, he may, on this account, pronounce them true; but they are true because they are consistent, and not because they have been revealed. This single consideration, that the English believer knows nothing of the original state of the Bible, is of itself sufficient to annihilate all his confidence. But this is not all; this book is said to be given by divine inspiration; but is it possible that inspiration can be either transferred, translated, altered, or revised? Certainly the very nature of the thing forbids it. If the scriptures be given by divine inspiration, their contents must be communicated to certain individuals by supernatural power. These individuals had no such power to transfer to other individuals with the same force of authority, the celestial information which they had received. If it were binding on the first persons who received it, it could not be equally so upon the second, for the nature and force of the communications were essentially destroyed. The first power that communicated was divine, the second was human; the first was incapable of error, the second deceptive and fallacious. If it were therefore to be admitted that any human beings were ever inspired, it would not follow that the result of that inspiration could be communicated with certitude or divine authority to any other minds. The idea of transferring celestial information received by supernatural means, is absurd and impossible; it is as impossible as that man could become a God, and exercise the attributes of the Divinity. The idea of translating a supernatural system of religion, is equally incorrect. The readers of such a system, even in the original languages, could not know that the things therein contained were inspired by God himself, if those few be accepted who were supposed to be the recipients of such sacred instruction; much less could the reader in subsequent ages be assured of the truth or validity of such translated doctrines. To render this system correct, and keep up the chain of divine connection, it is not only necessary that the first prophets and apostles should have been inspired, but that all the translators, transcribers, printers, and printers' boys, should have been inspired also. In deficiency of such arrangement, the Christian believer at the present day must be uncertain whether he believes in holy writ, or the imaginary conceptions and wild reveries of the human understanding. If inspiration be a thing founded in truth, there can be no occasion to alter or revise it. It is defect alone that creates the necessity of alteration and revision. If, therefore, the Bible was right at first, every alteration is a deviation from that rectitude; and, consequently, in proportion as the scriptures have been altered and revised in modern times, the Christian believer has been led astray; he has not believed in the real and true word of God. If the scripture was wrong at first, the faith of the primitive Christian was nothing more than a delusive error; in either of these cases we are thrown into a dilemma, from which clerical ingenuity alone will be able to extricate us. The last resort of the believer, must be to the authority and command of his Majesty, who has kindly interfered for the purpose of rendering divine and holy, a book, whose indecency and immorality shocks all common sense and common honesty.

CHAPTER V

Original Sin, Atonement, Faith, & a Christmas Discourse, Delivered in New York, Dec. 1796

This, my friends, we are told, is Christmas-day; and while the pious and learned divines of all Christendom are extolling the beauties, the excellencies, and the divinity of the Christian religion; while its doctrines are represented as the most pure and celestial, its morality exalted above that of any other ethical treatise, and the goodness of the Creator represented as demanding the most unreserved gratitude, and the highest affection of the human heart: while this absurd and cruel system is every where held up to admiration, as containing the height of divine perfection and the most unbounded displays of infinite benevolence; while an ignorant and astonished world are called upon to yield an unqualified credence to the mysterious dogmas of this mysterious religion; while, in a word, the thundering voice of the Christian world is proclaiming to the elect few the joys which are reserved as their unfailing portion, and damnation to the many who are unfortunately destitute of what they call saving and supernatural faith; be it our task to inquire into the truth or falsehood of these declarations. This inquiry shall be made without reference to any other principle than that of truth, or any other effect than that of the happiness of mankind. Elevated in our conceptions above every possible consideration resulting from hope or fear, and having truth only for our object, we shall proceed to an unreserved examination of this so much celebrated system of religion, called Christianity. The world has been so long in the habit of believing it to be true, that the mind seems to have lost all traces of independent investigation; a mental stupidity has taken possession of the human faculties, and liberal inquiry has been lost in the vortex of clerical authority. A general torpor has reigned for ages past, and it is now time to throw in our aid, to awaken the mental energy of intelligent beings. Let us proceed, then, to an unprejudiced discussion of the subject; and in order to do this with perspicuity, the following method shall be observed:—1st. We shall make some remarks concerning Jesus Christ. 2dly. We shall consider the doctrines of the Christian religion. 3dly. The morality of this religion. 4thly. The effects of the introduction of Christianity into the world.

With respect to the first proposition, we may observe, that among other strange and marvelous things contained in this scheme of religion, the conception of Jesus Christ is very singular and unnatural; he is ushered into the world in a manner neither credible nor cognizable by the human mind; he has a mother, it is true, but he has no father; for although the lineal descent is traced through many generations down to the person who ought to have been his father, yet the chain is here broken, and he is said to have been begotten by a ghost. To what purpose is this genealogy given, when the lineal descent is to be wholly destroyed in the conclusion of the scene? And after having destroyed it, and ascribed the conception to an unknown phantom, called the Holy Ghost, he is then said to be the eternal Son of the Father, that is, of the Creator and Preserver of the universe. If he is the only-begotten Son of the Father, how can he be the Son of the Holy Ghost? And if he was really begotten by this Ghost, what had the Father to do with this scene of debauchery? At any rate, what conception can the human mind form of this absurd and contradictory representation? This child, when born, appears to be a human being, and yet his is supernaturally begotten by two supernatural fathers, and he is as old as either of them. Sophistry and folly united cannot exhibit a greater specimen of nonsense and irrationality. This story of the virgin and the ghost, to say no more of it, does not wear the appearance of much religion; and it would not, it is presumed, be difficult in any age or country, to find a sufficient number of men who would pretend to be ghosts, if by such pretensions they could obtain similar favors, especially with the consoling reflection super added, of becoming the progenitors of the pretended Savior of a wicked and apostate world. How absurd and contradictory are the principles and the doctrines of this religion! In vain do its advocates attempt to cover this transaction with the machinery of ghosts and supernatural agents. The simple truth is, that their pretended Savior is nothing more than an illegitimate Jew, and their hopes of salvation through him rest on no better foundation than that of fornication or adultery.

But let us suppose that the mode of bringing him into the world was natural and consistent; what valuable purpose has been effected by it? There has been none, either in his conception, his birth, his life, or his death, unless the horrid cruelties, the murderous wars and devastation, which have disgraced the annals of the Christian world, can be considered as blessings to mankind. In every moral point of view, the world is infinitely worse, and so far as relates to their felicity, we may boldly assert, that wretchedness has been increased; yet this was the man who was to do away sin, and bring in an everlasting righteousness; this was the source whence innumerable benefits were to be derived; but, alas! wickedness and misery have been the continued and uniform result.

But to proceed,—What was the conduct of this person, called Jesus Christ? Was it like the conduct of a deity, or like that of an ignorant uninformed man? Was it the conduct of divine wisdom, or that of imbecility and distrustful apprehension? If this man, Jesus Christ, had really entered into a coalition with the Creator of the world, for the accomplishment of important purposes relative to the happiness of the human race; if the stipulation had been well understood by the two contracting parties, in the origin of the business; if the intelligent Creator of the world on his part, had asserted that there was no other mode of producing the benefits intended, than by the death of his only begotten Son, and the multiplicity of sufferings and calamities which necessarily resulted from so arduous and important an undertaking; and if, on the other hand, this pretended Son of God was apprized of the unavoidable evils which were connected with his mission; if all the previous arrangements and subsequent events had been well and clearly determined between them; and if the whole had been directed by infinite wis6dom, power, and goodness, what ought to have been the final effect of this splendid celestial embassy? Ought we not to conclude, that the general felicity of intelligent beings on the surface of the globe, must have been the unavoidable consequence? Are we not bound to suppose that a plan of operation formed in the cabinet of eternal wisdom, must have answered all the purposes which that wisdom was calculated to produce? Instead of this, how wretchedly are we disappointed? Vice is not destroyed, and the fears of future damnation are increased. Three infinite Gods have laboured in vain, and their united efforts have not been able to rescue mankind from endless torments. But further, why was not this pretended Savior exhibited to the world, the nature of his scheme, and extensive benefits of his mission? Was he uninformed, or was he incapable of communicating to intelligent beings the knowledge of a plan on which their eternal felicity depended? If, as is pretended, he had been God himself, or if he had been enlightened by the wisdom of the Creator, no progressive steps of science could be applicable to his condition. It could not be necessary for him to go to a school or academy in order to learn to read or write, and yet we have no evidence that he was capable of either, and the negative evidence on this point is almost conclusive, as to his want of common information. To have convinced the world of his supernatural conception and celestial mission, he ought to have written a moral and theological treatise, in which the principles of his mission should have been elucidated in a manner intelligible to every living creature, interested in the possession of such knowledge. But unfortunately for mankind, this has not been the case; all is doubt—all is uncertainty; and we are left to depend on the opinions and declarations of others, who seem to have known but little of the matter. They tell us an unconnected and inconsistent story, of the conception, the life, the death, and the resurrection of Jesus Christ; but they have no system, and their development of moral principles is partial, and inaccurate;

but the concluding scene of his life exhibits some information worthy of our impartial attention. In his last moments he cries out, "My God, my God, why hast thou forsaken me!" What conclusion is it natural to draw from this distressing exclamation? It appears to be this, that on the part of Jesus Christ, there was a virtual renunciation of his confidence in the Creator; and on the supposition that there was originally a concerted plan of execution well understood by both the parties, the fulfillment of it seems here to have been relinquished, and the beneficial effects annihilated. On the part of Jesus, it is saying, "I have been deceived in this undertaking. I did not expect that I should have been forsaken in this hour of my greatest distress; but I rested with confidence on eternal wisdom, for a timely escape from this wretched misfortune." On the part of the Father, there is a want of attention and support in this trying hour. He forsakes his beloved Son; he gives him up to the murderous fury of vindictive enemies; and neither the one nor the other of the parties exhibits that spirit of fortitude and constancy which might justly have been expected on so interesting an occasion. The reflecting mind concludes, therefore, that the whole is but a fiction, and that no such stipulation ever took place between the man Jesus Christ, and the Creator of the world.

We shall now proceed to an examination of the doctrines of the Christian religion, and compare them with the principles of a genuine and natural morality, the nature and character of man, and the perfections of the intelligent Creator of the universe. If the founder of this religion was destitute of authority in his mission, the doctrines which are applicable to him will fall of course; but so strong are the prejudices of mankind in favor of these doctrines, that it becomes necessary to expose the immorality of them before we can expect that they will be relinquished. The most important doctrines of this supposed celestial scheme, are those of original sin, atonement, faith, and regeneration. The first two of these are essentially immoral in their nature. The third, though considered as a virtue by Christians, has nothing in it either of merit or demerit, and the last being supernatural, is not cognizable by the faculties of the human mind. This strange and unnatural system, called the the Christian religion, commences the development of its dogmas, by the destruction of every principle of distributive justice. It makes the intelligent beings who are now in existence accountable for the errors and vices of a man who lived six thousand years ago; a man who, its advocates say, God created upright, free from every kind of impurity, and placed in a state of uniform happiness, with a strong natural propensity to the practice of every virtue, and an equally strong aversion to every vicious and immoral principle; created in the image of God himself, and possessing an unqualified attachment to celestial purity and goodness. This man, nevertheless, transgressed the divine law, and this solitary violation becomes temporarily and eternally fatal to the human race. Moral impurity assumes a new shape, and becomes transferable through successive generations. Though none of this man's descendants could possibly be partakers of this original criminality, they are, nevertheless, implicated in the consequences and effects of his primary apostasy. "They sinned with him, and fell with him, in his first transgression." This is the language of pious and learned divines, and of the rectitude of the principle we are not permitted to doubt, under pain of eternal damnation. But the truth compels us to assert, that this doctrine, called original sin, is, in the first place, totally impossible, and in the second place, that it is as immoral and unjust, as the Creator is righteous and benevolent. The virtues and the vices of intelligent beings are not of a transferable but of a personal nature. In a moral point of view, the amiable or useful qualities of one man cannot become those of another, neither can the vices of one be justifiably punished in the person of another. Every man is accountable for himself; and when he can take no cognizance of the intentions or actions of any other man, how can he be justly responsible for their injurious effects, or applauded for any benefits resulting from them? If Adam or any other man, who lived several thousand years ago, was guilty of an immoral conduct, what has that to do with the moral condition of the present generation? Is a man to become criminal before he has existed? or, is he to be criminated afterwards, by the immoral conduct of those who lived long before him? Has not every man errors enough of his own to answer for, without being implicated in the injurious consequences resulting from the bad conduct of his neighbor?

Shall there be no line of moral precision, by which human beings can be tried, condemned, or acquitted? It seems by the general tenor of this doctrine, that every rule of moral precision is here totally disregarded, and setting aside the want of justice, the whole business wears a farcical and ludicrous appearance. This original evil so destructive to the human race, commences by the eating of what is called the forbidden fruit. Whether the fruit was an apple, a peach, or an orange, is not material for us to know; if it was either the one or the other of these, and the fruit was good, there could be no harm in eating it, and if bad, let him take the consequence whose ignorance or temerity induced the action. But whether good or bad, whether eaten or not eaten, is nothing to us, and we are neither worse nor better for reading this foolish story. The moral impurity of the heart can bear no possible relation to the criminality of Adam, or any other man of that day or generation. Let Adam, therefore, and his partner Eve, together with the Devil and his snakes, attend to their own concerns, and if they have fallen into difficulties by their own follies and vices, let them extricate themselves as well as they are able. For myself, I have so much regard for all of them, that I hope they will not be damned for ever. For notwithstanding much noise and clamour has been raised, I think that neither party was so bad as the pious ambassadors of Heaven have represented them. The story is almost too foolish to deserve a serious examination. Let intelligent man study his own nature, and the passions of his heart, let him observe his relative condition and the springs of his action, and he will soon discern the causes of his calamity. He will find that disorganization or physical death is an unavoidable appendage of animal life. That the very construction of his nature insures the certainty of a subsequent derangement, and that the primary qualities of all sensitive beings gradually lead to dissolution. No organic perfectibility of animal existence has been discovered yet, which is capable of excluding the anticipation of decay through the progressive operations of physical causes upon the constitution; and perfect moral rectitude, though it were capable of extending the period, could not give ultimate durability to beings organized like ourselves; nevertheless, we are told that death(1) spiritual, temporal, and eternal, are the consequence of his primitive apostasy. By spiritual death is meant moral turpitude of the heart and character; but this in many beings obtains but partially, and is always the effect of personal infraction of moral principle, bearing no possible relation to Adam. By temporal death, is meant that death which experience teaches us to be the fate of every creature in the present world, and this death, though an essential ingredient in the constitution of nature, is foolishly and unphilosophically attributed to the sin of Adam. If Adam, previous to his supposed apostasy, had been thrown into a fire, or immersed in water, would not one of these elements have disorganized him, or the other have drowned him? or would he have returned from these trials with all the beauties of youth and vivacity in his appearance? If it be contended that he would, a constitution must then be attributed to him of which the human mind can form no conception. If it be admitted that he must have perished, temporal death can then no longer be attributed to the commission of moral evil, and it must be acknowledged as an essential property of our primary and physical organization; and that death is as natural as life in the order of the world. By eternal death, is meant a state of endless punishment; and so powerful is the influence of this sin of Adam upon the human race, that they all become liable to eternal torments on this account. One would have supposed that after having brought temporal death into the world by this transgression, and after having corrupted every moral principle of the human heart, the contrivers of the scheme might have been contented, without annexing to this crime any other fatal consequences; but fanaticism and superstition delight in murder, misery, and eternal fire; and to this flaming lake I wish them a speedy passage, never more to rise to insult the dignity, or destroy the happiness of the human race. To punish the temporary and finite crimes of a finite life with eternal fire, would be to relinquish every principle of distributive justice, and to act like an arbitrary and malevolent tyrant. All the sins that ever have been committed do not deserve this unlimited severity of punishment; and to attribute to one solitary infraction of a moral law these terrible consequences, is to lose sight of infinite benevolence and eternal justice. It is to represent the God of Nature as cruel and vindictive, and even less merciful than the majority of his creatures; it destroys all degrees in moral turpitude, and inflicts on a petty offender a punishment not merited by the greatest criminal. It is therefore evident that this original sin has not produced, and that it could not produce, any of the consequences which have been attributed to it, for death is one of the physical properties of our nature. Vice is the result of individual and personal infractions of moral law, and an eternal Hell is a bugbear of superstition, which has never answered, and never can answer, any valuable purpose even in preventing crimes. [1. See chapter on Death.]

Another important doctrine in the Christian religion is the atonement supposed to have been made by the death and sufferings of the pretended Savior of the world; and this is grounded upon principles as regardless of justice as the doctrine of original sin. It exhibits a spectacle truly distressing to the feelings of a benevolent mind, it calls innocence and virtue into a scene of suffering and reputed guilt, in order to destroy the injurious effects of real vice. It pretends to free the world from the fatal effects of a primary apostacy, by the sacrifice of an innocent being. Evil has already been introduced into the world, and in order to remove it, a fresh accumulation of crimes becomes necessary. In plain terms, to destroy one evil, another must be committed. To teach mankind virtue, they are to be presented with the example of murder; to render them happy, it is necessary to exhibit innocence in distress; to provide for them the joys of Heaven, wretchedness is to be made their portion on earth. To make them love one another, they must be taught that the Deity, regardless of this principle, voluntarily sacrificed his only begotten Son. In fine, to procure for intelligent beings the happiness suited to their nature, cruelty and vindictive malice must be exhibited for their contemplation. This doctrine presented in its true colors contains neither justice nor utility. Its principle is vicious, and its consequences are not beneficial. The reflecting mind which views the operation of causes and their natural effects, possesses a nice and accurate power of discrimination. Moral precision is an important object of attention, and although it traces the nature of the infinitely combined relations subsisting among beings of the same species, it cannot discern either the justice or the the utility of the relation which suffering virtue can bear to the destruction of moral evil. No connection can be discovered between the exclamations of expiring innocence, and the triumphant march of vice over an apostate world. Does the suffering of the virtuous man destroy the evil habits or propensities of him who is vicious and abandoned, especially when he is told that these sufferings are to annihilate his own crimes? Can this induce the mind to exhibit any efforts wearing the appearance of reformation? Does it not rather contribute to the practice of vice, from the belief that the burden and effect must be sustained by another person? Yet this is the true ground on which this scheme of atonement is promulgated. It is exhibited as a substitute for moral perfection. It teaches man that his own virtues are insufficient for his felicity; that the cultivation of his faculties, and the discovery and practice of moral truth, can never lead to substantial happiness. This must be obtained from the sufferings and expiring groans of the Deity himself. But even on Christian principles, what useful purpose has this atonement answered? Though the believers of this religion have sacrificed the God of Nature to gratify their pride, have they by this means accomplished their end? Have they established a sure foundation for the destruction of moral evil? Have they insured permanent happiness to every intelligent being? No; this desirable end is not completed. Sin, say they, is an infinite evil. Was the atonement infinite? Alas! No; for although Jesus Christ, who suffered, was equal to God himself, yet all of them acknowledge that it was the human, not the divine nature that partook of this suffering. If, therefore, it was the human nature only that suffered, this suffering could only make a finite atonement, and if the sin was infinite, this atonement could not reach its nature or destroy its effects; for to have done this, the atonement must have been commensurate with the evil to be destroyed; but as the one is finite, and the other infinite, no relation could have subsisted between them, and no beneficial effect has been or can be produced from it. This method of destroying evil is an unfortunate one; it is essentially unjust in its principles, and useless in its effects; it professes to sacrifice an infinite being, but it denies the possibility of this sacrifice producing any thing more than a finite atonement. If an atonement was necessary, it ought to have been as extensive and complete in its nature as the offences intended to be destroyed by its influence. But instead of this, every thing is reversed. According to believers themselves, this atonement has not reached the condition of more than one-tenth part of the human race. The efforts of Trinitarian wisdom have all failed, and notwithstanding the pretended good news of the Gospel, every living creature is destined to never-ending torment. The elect themselves are incapable of escaping eternal damnation, for without an atonement they cannot be saved, and the atonement that has been made is not equal to the crime committed. If, therefore, our hopes of salvation are to rest on this vicarious suffering, we shall be essentially disappointed, and endless misery must be the lot of man. Priests and fanatics of the world! is this your scheme of infinite benevolence? This your theme of divine eloquence? Is this the only way in which you can exhibit the perfections of your God, and adore his eternal wisdom? Are murder, carnage, and injustice, the objects in which you delight? Have you lost all attachment to moral virtue, all veneration for the dignity and faculties of your nature? Have you dismissed all respect for nature and for truth? Will you never learn wisdom from the book of Nature, will you never derive instruction from the permanency of her laws? Is it only among miracles, ghosts, and crucified Gods that you delight to walk? Oh! prejudiced and superstitious man, look at the splendid beauties of Nature, look at the vast machinery of the universe, and through these thou mayest discover the intelligent organizer of the whole, perfect in all his attributes, and worthy of thy adoration.

The next principle of discussion is, that of Christian faith; and this among the believers of this religion has been considered as a great virtue. But is this substantially true? What is the real meaning of the word "Faith?" It is necessary to inquire concerning its true definition, and from this inquiry we shall be able to draw a conclusion whether or not the principle of faith is meritorious. Faith is an assent of the mind to the truth of a proposition supported by evidence. If the evidence adduced is sufficient to convince the mind, credence is the necessary result; if the evidence be insufficient, belief becomes impossible. In religion, therefore, or in any other of the concerns of life, if the mind discerns that quantum of evidence necessary to establish the truth of any proposition, it will yield to the force and effect of the proofs which are produced; if, on the other hand, the intelligence of man does not discern the necessary influence of such evidence, infidelity will be the natural and unavoidable result. Why then is the principle of faith considered a virtue? If a man beholds the sun in its meridian splendor, and declares the truth of this exhibition, is he meritorious in making this acknowledgment? If any truth in nature is well substantiated and supported by the testimony of his mind or senses, does he deserve credit for his mental acquiescence? No. Why then have the Christian world annexed to this principle of belief any degree of merit? Is necessary acquiescence a virtue? Does man become entitled to praise for the acknowledgment of facts guaranteed by his senses, or essentially supported through the channel of his mental faculties? Does truth really exist in the system of nature? And is this truth discoverable by the operations of the human mind? And shall man, notwithstanding this, arrogate to himself a high degree of importance, for the rejection of the splendid testimonies which are exhibited for his contemplation? No; after a full display of evidence, the mind must yield to its necessary and unavoidable influence. When, therefore, the Christian religion represents faith as being meritorious, it loses sight of the natural operations of the human mind; it betrays an ignorance of nature, and becomes censurable by its deviation from the primary and essential arrangements. Yet in this holy book we are told, that "he that believeth not shall be damned." But what are we to believe? Are we to believe that the Creator of the universe is the parent and friend of the whole human race? Are we to believe that his wisdom acts in coincidence with general felicity, or operates on the ground of universal happiness? Are we to believe that the establishment of general laws is sufficient for the well-being of intelligent agents? Are we to believe the vast machinery of the universe to be under the guidance and direction of eternal perfection? Are we to believe that the primary principles of our nature are sufficient for our improvement and ultimate perfectibility? Are we to believe that the practice of moral virtue is essentially connected with the dignity and final improvement of the human species? Are we to believe that the establishment of good laws, and the exhibitions of moral energies, are essentially interwoven with the permanent happiness of sensitive creatures? No! We are not permitted to believe this. What then is Christian belief? What are the dogmas and principles to which we are required to give an unqualified credence? However painful it may be to declare it, they are of the following nature:—That the great Creator of the world sacrificed his only-begotten Son for the happiness of the human race; that he sent numerous prophets and apostles to teach and instruct mankind; that they were charged with the disclosure of every species of celestial knowledge, relative to the future felicity of intelligent beings; that they were unwearied in their attention to enlighten and inform the human race; that they exhibited every possible effort for the accomplishment of this desirable end, and all this to no valuable purpose; that man is to be criminated for the bad conduct of a person who lived 6,000 years ago; that he can be made happy only by a crucified God; that he can perform no virtue of himself, and yet, that without being perfectly holy, he cannot be happy; that he must give an unlimited credence to the greatest absurdities, and most palpable contradictions, and view the most immoral specimens of human actions as sanctioned by the Deity; that he must venerate the most senseless opinions, admire the most unexampled ignorance, and love the most detestable crimes; in fact, that he must believe in a book which contains, systematically considered, neither truth nor morality, neither purity of sentiment nor principle, neither propriety of arrangement, nor progression of human improvement; erroneous in all its primary establishments and vindictive in all its consequences; unjust in its origin and malevolent in all its subsequent movements; incorrect in its relations and impure in its intentions; destructive to science, an insult to morality, and essentially injurious to human felicity.

This then is Christian faith. Great God of Nature! Must we then renounce the justifiable exercise of all our faculties, in order to be happy? To attain felicity, is it necessary that we believe in contradictions? Must we deem cruelty one of the attributes of divinity?

Must the benevolent mind be called to the view of murder, in order to be fitted for the performance of its essential duties? Must injustice and revenge be interwoven with the morality of man? Shall we never be permitted to love truth, admire nature, and practice a pure and genuine morality? Oh, superstition! how much thou hast to answer for! thine influence has corrupted the faculties of man, debased his heart, and rendered wretched the whole human race. Thou hast spread ruin, misery, and devastation over a beautiful and productive earth, and thou art deserving of the curses of every intelligent being in every part of the universe.

Another divine doctrine of this divine religion is that of regeneration. This doctrine appears to be scarcely deserving of a serious consideration. When the mind of man takes cognizance of the operations of nature, it discerns no effect which can possibly include an event of this sort. We behold the renovations and alterations in the material world; we observe the principles and progression of gradual decay, in all its essential and relative movements, and we recognize the benefits which result from the principle of mutability. The principles of disorganization and reproduction, are every where discoverable in the works of nature, but no justifiable analogy can possibly be drawn from this view of the subject. The renovation in the material world bears no resemblance to the Christian principle of regeneration. The one is cognizable and rests on natural grounds, the other is inconsistent with the knowledge derived from experience. The human mind, through the channels of its observation, discovers the means of perpetuating the species; but this mental regeneration bears no relation to these progressive means of production. It is necessary, therefore, that we examine what is meant by this unintelligible principle, called regeneration. It seems to be almost impossible to obtain any accurate or definite idea, from the representation which is given concerning this pretended and important change. Those who are the subjects of it profess themselves to be incapable of disclosing its real movements or genuine operations. If it were an event, of which the human mind had any real knowledge or experience, one would suppose that the faculty of communication would render it in some measure intelligible to others; but enthusiasm delights in mystery, and by embracing this doctrine, has given a powerful specimen of its fanaticism and importance. It pretends to the acquisition of something, concerning which, it can exhibit no adequate idea or useful information. It is a mysterious and inexplicable change of the mind, pretendedly for the better, and yet no valuable purposes seem to be answered by this divine renovation. The being, who is the subject of it, becomes neither the wiser nor the better; he is not the wiser, because he can give no proofs of additional knowledge; his disposition is not amended, for his conduct continues the same. For the truth of this observation we may appeal to experience. Are the saints of the world more just, more honest, more benevolent, or charitable, than those who make no pretensions to supernatural grace? Is their heart or their temper of mind ameliorated? Is their conduct in stricter conformity with useful or exalted virtue? Do they sympathize more with the unfortunate, or exhibit greater specimens of genuine benevolence? Is the heart tranquillized, the mind improved, and their actions more consistent with the invariable principles of rectitude? Have they diminished human misery, or improved the condition of human nature? No! Where then is the utility of this thing called regeneration? If the heart be not improved, the mind cultivated, or morality extended in the sphere of its influence, no advantage has resulted from this pretended change. If any benefit has been derived, it ought to be shown; but the history of the Christian world forbids the attempt.

But further, the performance of the duty which is assigned to the being called the Holy Ghost, seems to have been attended to in a manner not discernible by the highest faculties of the human mind. If this being had really undertaken the moral renovation of the human species, he ought to have rendered it universal, and explained its operations on cognizable grounds. But no such thing having been done, the rational conclusion must be, that the whole is a delusion. Indeed the New Testament representation of this affair bears an unequivocal and unmeaning appearance. It is there declared, "Except a man be born again, he cannot see the kingdom of God." And when Nicodemus makes the rational inquiry how such an event could possibly happen, he is put off with an evasive answer, (John chap. 3.) "Nicodemus saith unto him, how can a man be born when he is old? Can he enter the second time into his mother's womb, and be born? Jesus answered, verily I say unto thee; except a man be born of water and of the spirit, he cannot enter into the kingdom of God. Marvel not that I said unto thee, ye must be born again. The wind bloweth where it listeth, and thou hearest the sound thereof, but canst not tell whence it cometh, and whether it goeth, so is every one that is born of the spirit. Nicodemus answered and said unto him, how can these things be? Jesus answered and said unto him, Art thou a master of Israel, and knowest not these things? Verily, verily, I say unto thee, we speak that we do know, and testify that we have seen, and ye receive not our witness. If I have told you earthly things, and ye believe not, how shall ye believe if I tell you of heavenly things?" etc. From this passage it is evident that Jesus, who made the answer to Nicodemus, knew nothing of the nature of this marvelous change. Being born of water and of the spirit is a phrase without meaning; what ideas can this possibly convey to the mind? but the advocates of this doctrine contend that one part of this sentence relates to baptism, and the other to the influence of the Holy Ghost. This does not mend the matter, neither does it exhibit any new species of information; for what has baptism to do with the moral condition of man? Can water, externally applied, destroy internal moral turpitude? If human vices could be cured through this channel, the more rational efforts for the renovation and improvement of our character would become unnecessary. But it is clearly discernible, that as vice is a violation of moral law, the way to remedy the mischiefs resulting from this violation, is not to pour water on the face, which can have no possible influence on the mind, but to return to uniform conduct, consistent with the primary principles of moral virtue. And further, to be born of the Spirit, being unintelligible, and without any beneficial effect, is equally ridiculous and absurd. The comparison of this regeneration with the blowing of the wind, exhibits nothing but the ignorance of him who made it. Indeed the principle on which the doctrine rests, is so unnatural and so destitute of any valuable effects, that it is unworthy of further consideration.

The next point of examination is the morality of the Christian religion. On this head, the advocates of this revealed system have made a mistake injurious to themselves, by extolling its morality above that of any other moral treatise; they have provoked inquiry and comparison, and the result serves only to diminish the pretended excellence of their scheme. It is not denied that this religion contains some good moral maxims. But it is denied that it contains any thing like a pure "system" of genuine morality. Its moral maxims are but thinly interspersed, and they are inaccurate and incomplete, trifling, and often without utility, destitute of justifiable application to the moral condition of intellectual life. All morality that is genuine, is drawn from the nature and condition of rational beings. It is calculated to preserve and augment their happiness, to raise and extend the dignity and utility of social existence. It assumes for its basis, the genuine principles of reciprocal justice, and an extensive benevolence. While it regards the felicity of others, it also regards the preservation of our own life and happiness. But the moral doctrine concerning injuries, contained in the Christian religion, is not established upon a principle of this mutual nature, but solicits an accumulation of insult, by commanding us after being smitten on one cheek to turn the other also. This is sacrificing the dignity of our character, and inviting fresh injuries. It is surrendering up the manly part of our nature, into the hands of him who is sure to trample it under foot. And again it is said, "If any man will sue thee at the law, and take away thy coat, let him have thy cloak also;" that is, after thine enemy hath unjustly taken away a part of thy property, it becomes thy duty to bestow upon him the remainder. If thy coat is already gone, thou must give away the remainder of thy garments, and go naked thyself. If thine enemy do thee all possible injury, thou must in return exercise towards him sincere love and affection. If he persecute thee, thou shouldst bless him for his curses and persecutions. In short, to comply with the spirit of this morality, we must invert the order of nature, and bestow on crimes and continued abuse, the most endearing affections of our heart. Where is the believer who puts this morality into practice? It is not considered by every one as merely theoretical. Have you who are believers in this system, coats and other garments to bestow, in order to comply with its injunctions? Are you willing to surrender your natural dignity, to sink your nature to a level of a spaniel, in order to become a true Christian? And can you, with any appearance of truth and justice, advocate the purity and celestial nature of this species of moral maxims? It may reasonably be presumed that if one coat had been obtained through the channel of a law suit, another law suit would be necessary in order to obtain the cloak. And thus this celestial morality would become the cause of endless litigation. But if we should accede to the truth of the assertion, that all the maxims held as moral by the professors of Christianity, were really and truly so, this would not prove the celestial origin of their religion. For if we attribute to them all the excellence which is contended for, they still fall below ancient and modern dissertations on this subject. This religion does not draw its morality from the right source. But the correct, the elegant, the useful maxims of Confucius, Antoninus, Seneca, Price, and Volney, beautifully display its principles from the physical and moral organization of intelligent beings. The writings of these men are in the hands of the public, and may be perused by every one whose prejudices do not forbid it, and when examined with a spirit of candour, they will rise far superior to the boasted morality of the Christian system. But when the numerous, cruel, and immoral maxims contained in the Bible, are placed in the balance, they greatly outweigh all its genuine morality, and the influence of this religion upon the human heart and human actions verifies the remark.

But of this we shall speak in the next division of the subject, which is the consideration of the effects produced by the introduction of the Christian religion into the world.

When the human mind takes a retrospective view of past ages, through the mirror of history; when it calls up to its contemplation, the murderous devastations, the horrid wars and cruelties which have desolated the Christian world; when it beholds the fagot every where lighted up for the destruction of man; when gibbets, imprisonment, and persecutions are presented on every quarter; when it sees domestic peace and tranquility tortured and almost annihilated, malevolence and sectarian spirit enkindling the most unbridled resentments to disturb the benevolent sentiments of the human heart; when, in fact, all Christendom exhibits a spectacle shocking to humanity, the weeping voice of Nature cries aloud, and demands a disclosure of the causes which have produced this general misery and distress. It asks, in the name of Reason and Truth, whence all these calamities, whence these innumerable evils that have overwhelmed and laid waste a beautiful and productive earth? Where is the source of these human misfortunes? Where the fountain whence these miseries proceed? Righteous God of Nature! What questions are these to ask in the face of the Christian church? But however painful the task, truth compels us to declare, that to this "holy" religion they are to be attributed. In this wonderful system of divine benevolence, we must seek for the origin.

"Does the God of Nature then require devastation for homage, or conflagration for sacrifice? Would he have groans for hymns? Murderers to worship him, and a desert and ravaged world for his temple? Yet such, holy and faithful generations, are your works! These the fruits of your piety! You have massacred the people, reduced cities to ashes, destroyed all traces of cultivation, made the earth a solitude, and you demand the reward of your labors. For myself, I solemnly affirm by all laws, human and divine, by the laws of the human heart, that the hypocrite and the deceiver shall be themselves deceived. The unjust man shall perish in his rapacity, and the tyrant in his usurpation; the sun shall change his course, before folly shall prevail over wisdom and science, before stupidity shall surpass prudential economy in the delicate art of procuring to man his true enjoyments, and of building his happiness on a solid foundation." (1) [1. Volney's "Ruins."]

We now proceed to exhibit, more particularly, the fatal effects of the Christian religion, relative to science, to morality, and human happiness. In vain do the advocates of this system contend for its beneficial effects as it regards these three principles. Science has been suppressed, morality insulted, and human happiness partially destroyed.

If the introduction of this religion into the world had been calculated to accelerate the progress of human improvement, or to render mankind wiser and happier, history should have recorded the progressive steps of this accumulating knowledge. But instead of this, the reverse stands confessed on the face of the record. When did the light of science begin to extend its benign influence over the surface of the globe? Was it at the commencement of the Christian era, and did it keep pace with the progressive belief of the Christian doctrines? Did the mind of man receive any impulse beneficial to the cause of knowledge, when this religion was first promulgated; and did the extension of useful information bear any justifiable relation to the diffusion of Christian principles? Did the world become either wiser or better after this religion had unfolded its genuine effects for more than fifteen centuries? Was this the cause of giving energy to the intellectual faculties of man? Were the genuine principles of science, which are contained in the system of nature, displayed and manifested by the establishment of this religion? In a word, has Christianity enlightened the world? No! But it has served as a means to suppress useful knowledge; for neither the commencement nor progressive establishment of this religion has contributed to useful information. If science were connected with the establishment and belief of Christianity, its advancement ought to have kept pace with the accelerated operation of its cause. But the reverse is the fact, for while the Christian religion has its greatest effect on the human mind, the useful branches of science were totally neglected, and the world was buried in the most profound darkness and ignorance; but when the physical energy of man roused itself from its slumbering and depressed condition, it took cognizance of primary principles, and discovered truth from the invariable laws of nature. While the mind was under the influence of clerical authority, independent reflection was effectually suppressed, and fear had destroyed all scientific efforts. Geography, astronomy, and natural philosophy, in short, the whole science of physics was denied the privilege of liberal inquiry and discussion. Religion affirmed the earth to be as flat as a trencher, and he who denied this assertion, was charged with a damnable heresy. Religion denied the existence of the Antipodes, and Genius trembled beneath its threatening rod. Religion inverted the whole order of nature, and truth and science had no safe or beneficial appeal. Religion pronounced damnation to the philosophic inquirer, and he sought tranquillity in the dark abodes of ignorance, or the suppression of useful knowledge. In short, religion governed by terror, and the mind of man painfully submitted to its destructive influence, till, at length, wearied and distressed by this degrading authority, it boldly asserted its own natural dignity and independence, and dared to draw its knowledge from the pure fountain of nature. As knowledge began to increase, the influence of the Christian religion and the authority of the church were seen to diminish; and as in the one case, ignorance kept pace with the promulgated influence of this religion, so in the other, science has kept pace, and extended itself in proportion to the destruction of Christian influence and authority; and where at this period there is the most science, there the least credence is given to revealed religion; where the principles of physics, morality, and politics have been most clearly understood, there the least respect is paid to this system of fanaticism and superstition. In short, they are incompatible with each other, and it may be confidently maintained that the world must either retrograde to a state of darkness, or that the belief of the Christian religion must become wholly extinct. If the mind of man should progressively advance towards a state of perfectibility, this system of religion, so injurious to its researches and so incompatible with the dignity and happiness of his nature, must be forever annihilated and destroyed. If, on the other hand, this unnatural scheme of ethics is permitted to retain its mischievous influence, the highest and best hopes of the philanthropist must be abandoned, and ignorance and misery become the lot of mortals. But God forbid that this should ever be the case. The benevolent mind, while reflecting on the subject, entertains a strong hope, that the reverse will obtain, and that the world will ultimately become virtuous and happy.

Again, this religion claiming with so much imperious austerity, celestial origin, has not been less injurious to the cause of morality, than to that of science. Its fundamental principles are of a nature destructive to all moral virtue, its doctrines openly disavow all benefit resulting from the practice of a genuine morality. Faith, atonement, and supernatural grace are the essential requisites of eternal happiness, and these have nothing to do with the mental or moral energies of our nature. The cultivation of our minds, the improvement of our faculties, and the performance of moral duties, by which alone man can expect or deserve to enjoy permanent felicity, are not considered as the proper means of acquiring it; but a blind an unintelligible faith, a mysterious and inexplicable belief in carnage and murder, are to become the objects of our highest admiration! "Not of works," says Paul, (the apostle of fanaticism and superstition) "lest any man should boast." And again, "It is not of him that willeth, nor of him that runneth, but of God that sheweth mercy." When maxims such as these are fundamental in any system of religion, what beneficial effects can result from it? It goes to the destruction of all moral effects. It represents man as incapable of performing any virtuous action. "For of yourselves ye can do nothing," is another maxim of this "holy religion." If man then can do nothing, nothing ought to be required of him; and if he is capable of practicing moral virtue, he ought to receive his reward. But inspiration teaches, that he ought to depend on the merit of another, and fanaticism cries aloud, that in Jesus alone you have hope; when the truth is, that neither the hopes, the welfare, or the happiness of man, can bear any possible relation to Jesus Christ or his opinions. Man is a being possessed of certain powers and faculties, and it is only through the justifiable exercise of these that he can be happy. But when he is taught to believe that his highest moral efforts can avail nothing; that he is completely under condemnation, in consequence of the imputed sin of him who lived six thousand years ago; that he can be relieved from the effects of this primary apostacy, only by the murder of an innocent person; that he can lay claim to this relief only through the channel of supernatural grace and divine aid; in fact, that of himself, he can do nothing; when he is taught to believe all this, what inducement can remain to the practice of virtue? There is none, and the mind is left to the gloomy anticipation of eternal fire. Was this religion instituted for the benefit and improvement of man? And do its professors deny him the power and beneficial results of moral exertions? Do they call him to virtuous activity for the purpose of insulting the useful energy of his nature? Do they in one breath represent him as an intelligent being, and in the next degrade him to the condition of a beast or a devil? It may be pronounced with certainty, that morality or real virtue can never be promoted by a scheme of religion containing such contradictions and absurdities, and that human enjoyment has been essentially diminished by the promulgation of such unnatural principles. Since it has already been shown that the Christian religion has been destructive to science and to morals, it seems almost unnecessary to make any observations on its relation to general happiness; for since the happiness of man depends essentially on the possession of knowledge and the practice of virtue, whatever injures these must be detrimental to his true felicity. The descriptions given in this religion of the character and conduct of the Almighty, are shocking to the reflections of the benevolent mind; they represent the Creator of the world, not as the friend, but as the enemy of man; as a being agitated by passions, and acting capriciously for the gratification of his own resentment; sometimes he is said to be merciful, at other times cruel and vindictive; sometimes just, at other times malevolent and revengeful; sometimes permanent and immutable in his actions and designs, at other times changeable, and to have repented of what he had previously determined to perform; at one time unbounded in his love, at another time unlimited in his fury and vengeance; sometimes the God of peace, at other times the God of wars and battles; now mild and peaceable, the next moment angry and resentful. "In short, this Christian God is ever at variance with himself," and in him no genuine confidence can be reposed. Can any one then be happy who trusts to a being of this description? To one who is imperfect, unstable, passionate, and revengeful? To a being who has, in fact, no uniformity of conduct, no system of action, and no immutability of procedure? No! Those who place their confidence here must be wretchedly disappointed, and an agitated mind will be their unavoidable portion. Yet to all this is added, the fear of an eternal Hell, as the certain and inevitable lot of nine-tenths of the human race. To say, therefore, that this religion has made mankind happy, is to disregard all the operations of the human heart, and the most justifiable hopes of the human mind.

Man! If thou wouldst be happy, thou must come home to Nature, admire her splendid beauties, develop truth from the permanence of her laws, cultivate real virtue, improve and exalt thy character, extend the sphere of thy utility, and invariably adhere to the practice of a pure and genuine morality.

CHAPTER VI

Origin of the Earth

Supernatural religion has been fertile in inventing systems concerning the origin of the world. The period that has been assigned to its duration has been extremely different among different nations of the earth, and has been limited or extended by theological authority. The Chinese records ascribe to the earth a duration of more than 20,000 years, and according to the opinions of some, of more than 40,000 years. These opinions are controverted by Christian believers, because, according to their sacred writings, the age of the earth is only about 6,000 years. Every opinion on this subject, which is supported by a popular and supernatural theology, is maintained with a tenacity which fanatic dogmatism never fails to inspire. It is, no doubt, a matter of curious inquiry when and by what means the earth was produced, what important changes it has undergone, and by what means these changes have been effectuated, and what will be their final result upon the modification and existence of the earth. While we inquire into the origin of the earth, we are also naturally led to the idea of the other extreme, and are solicitous to ascertain the ultimate extent of its duration. It is, however, a subject of vast difficulty, and involved in so much darkness and uncertainty, that it will probably always be impossible to reduce to absolute certitude any philosophical ideas upon this abstruse and difficult case. One thing, however, is certain, that if philosophy be ignorant upon the origin of the earth, theology, from the nature of its character, must be still more ignorant; philosophy investigates with patient and temperate perseverance, while theology is impelled by the gales of ranting enthusiasm. The latter is certain, without evidence, and the former is in doubt because it is deficient in evidence. When it is asserted by Christian believers, that without the Bible we should know nothing of the beginning or the end of this world, what do they say more than this, that we must take the authority and declaration of a theological book for absolute and positive truth, that assertion must supply the place of evidence; the ignorance of antiquity is to be preferred to the science of modern times; the decisions of the church ought to have more weight than the demonstration of intellect; that the mythology of every nation should be put into the balance against the strength of human judgment, and a comprehensible development of moral and physical laws. The earth which we inhabit occupies a station in that vast system which is presented to our view in the regions of space; it is the residence of beings whose powers are inadequate to a comprehension of all those vast objects which surround them; it is this ignorance that has induced the necessity of so many false and whimsical conjectures concerning the origin of the world.

There is, however, in this case one substantial consideration, to which we ought to direct our reflections. It is among the philosophical truths which cannot be controverted, that nothing can never become something, and that something can never become nothing. If this truth be applied to the present case, we shall have in part a solution of the difficulty, so far as it relates to the existence of the materials of which the earth is composed; but modification and local situation in the planetary system will constitute another part of the inquiry. Christian philosophers themselves have acceded to the axiom, that from nothing, nothing can be made; if this be true, as it clearly is, the eternal duration of the earth, in some form or other, will follow as a necessary consequence. It is declared in the 1st chapter of Genesis, that in the beginning God created the Heaven and the earth. But we are not told from what materials, or in what manner this work was performed. One thing, however, is remarkable in the account, that there were three days and three nights before the creation of the sun, which is the sole cause of day and night. This proves that Moses, or whoever wrote the 1st chapter of Genesis, was neither a good world-maker, nor a good astronomer. If the whimsical and incongruous opinions of theologists were to be credited, every part of the physical universe would be distorted, and all the useful discoveries òf philosophy would be destroyed by a single dash of authority. Moses makes day and night without the existence of the sun; Joshua stops the course of the sun; and the author of the gospel of St. Matthew precipitates the stars from their celestial condition, and causes them to descend upon the earth with as little difficulty "as if they had been so many pebble stones." It is not in the fanciful reveries of religionists that we are to expect to discover physical truth; the smallest frantic impulse is sufficient to overturn the beauty and harmony of Nature, and there is scarcely a religious zealot on earth who would not sacrifice natural truth to the phrenzy of his enthusiasm. When the temperate philosopher asserts that it is probable, in his view of the subject, that the earth has existed from all eternity, the Christian fanatic rises in all the power of holy and vindictive resentment, as if the question, in its ultimate tendency, involved the best interest of moral existence, and all the practical considerations of human life. Progressive investigation upon this subject will constantly be attended with a diminution of respect for theological opinions; but a doctrine once established in "supernatural religion" is henceforth to be denominated absolutely true and infallible; the most abstract speculations of a philosophical kind are damnable heresies, and the authors and supporters of them destined hereafter to experience the vindictive fury and unrelenting vengeance of the Jewish and Christian God.

The eternal duration of the earth, in some form or other, is rendered certain, by the essential properties of matter; whatever does exist must have existed from all eternity, and must, from its very nature, continue to exist for ever. Creation and annihilation, so far as these words are applied to the essence of things, are words without meaning, but so far as they are applied to a specific modification, they are intelligible and universal. Experience bears testimony to this solemn truth; but if the earth existed from all eternity, did it always hold the same relative position in regard to the sun and other planets? This is a question that can receive only a partial and probable solution, nor is it of importance to the true interest of philosophy that it should engage any high degree the attachment and energy of human intellect. The productions on the surface of the globe constitute, in some small degree, the foundation of ingenuous conjecture. The vivifying influence of the sun seems to be an operating cause, without which vegetation and life would be unknown; in the present condition of the earth, the effect of the sun is clearly discovered, and the productions which we behold are the result of its celestial power. Men exist, large animals of various species also exist, together with all subordinate exhibitions of physical energy. Procreation and reproduction of specific kind and class are the invariable laws of Nature. But the question of the greatest difficulty is that which relates to the origin of the first and most powerful kind of animals that exist upon the earth; the position which the globe at present holds in relation to the sun does not warrant us in the conclusion, that either man or the larger kinds of animals in brute creation could have resulted from this position. The same power that formerly produced them would be able to produce them still, and in addition to the ordinary process of reproduction, we should have a right to expect new beauties and wonders, equal, at least, to the most excellent which we now behold. This, however, is not the case, and the fair deduction on the ground of philosophy, is, that the relative position of the earth and sun must formerly have been different from what it is at present, and that it is upon a hypothesis of this kind that we are to seek for a solution of the highest difficulties with which we are presented in the animal world.

There is one other idea of analogical weight in the discussion of this part of the subject. Nature is every where periodical in her exertions and energies; she is susceptible of fatigue and lassitude, and her most powerful operations are followed by proportionate debility and inactivity. It is therefore possible in the order of Nature, that the most powerful animals might have been the result of an inconceivable exertion, to which Nature for millions of years after might have been totally incompetent. Among the human species there is evidently a great diversity of external appearance; the white and the black man are as different in some other respects, as they are in the colour of their skin; the long straight hair of the one, and the curled wool of the other, is a verification of this remark. Both races are intelligent, and it is presumed that the intellectual powers are not in any essential degree dissimilar. Improvement has made more difference than Nature, and the immoral opinion, that the whites have a right to enslave the blacks, is a complete abandonment of the principle of recipro-cal justice, and a violation of the fundamental laws of Nature. The only consideration which induced the mention of this subject, was to show, that it is probable that Nature has, at dif-ferent times, made great exertion in the work of creation or production, and that from man down to the lowest insect, a graduated modification of physical energy has been exhibited throughout a past eternity. It will be then inquired, whether this conjecture can be analogized with the idea of new pro-ductions in the planetary system? The answer to this inquiry must be given unequivocally in the negative. The axiom, that from nothing, nothing can be made, here applies with correct and indubitable force, and unless comets or planets interfere and derange each other's existence, there can be no new pro-duction; and even in such a case, it would be form alone that was new, and not essence and matter.

The changes that are exhibited in Nature are infinitely diversified, and the causes of these changes not clearly to be discovered. The mass of existence must remain for ever the same; but its modifications will vary throughout infinite space, and through all the successive periods of the eternal duration of time, or, to speak more correctly, through the progression of an interminable futurity. The whole mass of material existence is to us infinite, or at least incomprehen-sible. To its extent in the regions of space no limits can be assigned, and to its duration, anterior or subsequent, we can fix no period. The most probable conclusion resulting from the nature of matter, and the stability of physical laws, is, that the universe has existed from all eternity, and that its duration hereafter will be endless. Upon the earth all the different kinds of animals and all the individuals of each kind are seen in succession to die and dissolve into Nature; it is from this inferred, that death is a universal law so far as it relates to all the productions of earth. But we cannot analogize these facts with the planetary system[1]. We have never seen a planet die or dissolve into the vast ocean of space, we have therefore no good reason to believe that any such event will ever take place. If such a fact had been discovered in one single instance, it would be strong analogical evidence, that the same fate would ultimately overtake all the vast orbs which fill the unlimited regions of space, or that universal death is a universal law of Nature. The constancy of existence, and the immutability of physical laws, will, however, be a sufficient consolation to timid minds, apprehensive of a final dissolution of the beautiful system of the material world. Human nature may repose in these laws the utmost confidence, they will probably operate with "divine" energy throughout an endless futurity.

---

[1]Since the days of Elihu Palmer, astronomers have documented the dissolution of stars and their planets. However, it is also documented that the material sent out through space by the explosion of the stars goes on to form new stars, planets and life forms.

CHAPTER VII

Universal Deluge

The highest delight of theology is the destruction of the beauty, order, and harmony of the universe. A world regularly existing from all eternity, and continuing so to exist through an endless futurity, would be, in the estimation of supernatural theology, an object of disgust. To nourish the superstitious pride and folly of man, it is necessary to derange, overturn, and destroy the splendid beauties and majestic grandeur of the vast empire of Nature. Not content with the scheme of prediction, whose fulfillment including the ultimate dissolution of the earth, Superstition conceived it was necessary to retrace and discover in the history of past ages, an event equally distressing and terrific. For this purpose the story of the universal deluge was contrived, in which all the animals on the surface of the earth, a select number only excepted, fell a sacrifice to the vindictive vengeance of the Jewish God. The nature and details of this story are exposed to strong objections, and by an examination of the Bible account, the inconsistency and even impossibility of the case will be discovered. It will also appear by recurrence to the law of nature, that such an event is in no shape whatever deserving of human credence. The law of fluids and the deficiency of water render it physically impossible that the whole globe should be over-flowed at one and the same time. It is well known, that water always seeks its level; where the equilibrium is destroyed, there will be instantly a powerful effort to restore it. If, there-fore, the water was elevated sufficiently high to cover the high-est mountains, the seas would become dry, a vast cavity would be formed below, and the waters would be precipitated with inconceivable fury and force to supply the cavities below, and re-establish the consistent harmony of nature. The mountains of Andes, in South America, by far the most exalted land upon the surface of the earth, is, at the point of Chimberazo, 20,000 feet above the common surface of the ocean. There is, there-fore, a great deficiency of water to answer the purposes of a universal deluge. For as by the law of fluids, water uniformly seeks its level, it is necessary that all around the globe the water should be raised 20,000 feet, otherwise the American Andes would not have been covered, and the deluge would not have been universal. Let any one calculate what a vast quantity of water would have been necessary to have covered the whole earth to such a height, and he will soon discover the absurdity of this marvelous account, and still more marvelous event, related in the book of Genesis. To say that God created such a vast body of water for the sole purpose of drowning the world and all the creatures which he made in it, and afterwards anni-hilated it, is to assert, in the first place, that which is impos-sible, and throw upon the moral character of God a sarcasm, at which man ought to be ashamed, at which he ought to blush and be confounded. The account which is given of the deluge, subjects itself to strong suspicion of incorrectness and want of truth. It is impossible that the ark or any other vessel that every was built, could have contained all the animals which are said to have taken refuge in it. This ark, according to the Bible description of it, was in length about 525 feet, in breadth 87 1/2 feet, and in height 52 1/2 feet. It is easy to perceive, that a vessel of such dimensions had not the capacity of containing the numbers, and all the various kinds of animals which are said to have been rescued from the fatal effects of this general deluge. It is in vain that the advocates of this wonderful event fly to miracles, or the operations of supernatural powers. Miracle on miracle must have been performed, the nature of things perverted, her laws wholly changed, and the immutability of the divine character completely annihilated, before it could be possible for the human mind to accede to the truth of this marvelous event. Some curious and philosophical observations concerning the deluge, taken from Emmerson, a British writer, are here subjoined:

"Concerning the cause of this flood, some suppose it brought about by natural causes; and others, by nothing less than a divine power. Those that are for natural causes, imagine a comet to have passed near the earth at that time, and by its approach to have raised a very strong tide, which would increase as the comet approached earth. The effect of this would be, that this great tide would lay all places under water, and would consequently drown all the inhabitants so far as it reached. That such a cause as this is capable of producing this dismal effect, is very evident. For if so small a body as the moon, at the distance of sixty of the earth's semi-diameters, be able to raise a strong tide in the ocean, of twelve or fifteen feet high, a comet as big as the earth, and coming very near it would raise a prodigious tide, capable of overflowing all that side of the earth which is next to the comet, and also the opposite side. But then this could not drown all places at once; for at the quadratures, or in those places which have the comet in their horizon, they would have as great an ebb, but then it would have this effect, to overflow and drown all places successively. For this huge spheroid of water, always pointing towards the comet, would by the earth's rotation pass over all the countries of the world; and, therefore, in the space of twenty-four hours, the whole earth would be involved in water, and all animals as effectively destroyed as if the water staid 150 days upon the earth, especially as the earth must needs make several rotations after this manner, before it could get clear of this disturbing force of the comet. The natural and necessary effect of all this would be, that by such a prodigious and rapid motion of this vast body of water round the earth in twenty- four hours, all plants and trees must be torn up by the roots, and carried along with the current; all buildings demolished; the rocks, hills, and mountains dashed to pieces, and torn away; all the product of the sea, as fishes, shells, teeth, bones, etc. carried along with the flood, and thrown upon the earth, or even to the tops of mountains, promiscuously with other bodies; hardly anything could be found strong enough to withstand its force. In such a case as this, it would be impossible for any ark to live, or the strongest man-of-war to exist upon the surface of the ocean."

The arguments, physical and moral, against an event of this kind, are strong and conclusive. Nature is incompetent to any such exhibition, and the moral perfections of Deity forbid it. The flood is therefore a chimera, and one of the theological errors contained in the Bible system of religion. If no other errors of greater magnitude or more pernicious consequences were to be found in this "holy" book, it would be an object rather of pleasant amusement than of severe remark and condemnation.

CHAPTER VIII

Christian Wonders

The truth of a book is always to be suspected in proportion as it deviates from consistency or the general laws of nature. The story of the deluge, which was considered in the previous chapter, is followed in the "Holy Bible" by a relation of other marvelous circumstances, which necessarily create, in all candid minds, extreme doubts of the validity or rectitude of such writings. The wonders that are unfolded in the Old Testament, may, with propriety, be denominated Christian, since it is by a union of the two books that Christian doctors have constituted the essence and doctrines of revealed religion. If this book, which is considered as divine, had displayed with clearness, dignity, and solemnity, the character of the Creator; if the principles of reciprocal justice, and genuine morality, had been developed and marked with precision; if fact had been substituted in the room of fable, it would not have been an object of censure and condemnation, and the ridiculous and marvelous accounts, which in the Old Testament make up a considerable part of the book, would never have been presented to the human understanding as objects of veneration, belief, and attachment.

The destruction of the cities of Sodom and Gomorrah by fire and brimstone precipitated from Heaven in the form of rain; the blowing down the walls of Jericho with rams' horns, by the triumphant march of the priesthood round the city; the marvelous and frightful story of the witch of Endor; the woeful condition of Daniel in the den of lions; the hot sultry situation of Shadrach and his two companions in the fiery furnace; together with the unnatural and hopeless abode of poor Jonah in the belly of the whale; all these are specimens of that miserable and disgusting extravagance with which this "Holy Bible" is everywhere replete.

These are a few out of the number of that long catalog of foolish detail for which the scriptures of the Old and New Testament are so remarkable. If any man of the present day, who writes for the instruction and benefit of mankind, were to interlard his works with such idle, extravagant, and useless stories, he would be considered in a state of insanity, and his writings would be contemned even by Christian believers themselves. A rain of fire and brimstone is impossible in the order of nature, and inconsistent with the moral perfection of that Being who governs the world. In throwing down the walls of Jericho, there is something in the detail of the story which, in the first place, is calculated to excite in human nature sentiments of humor and ridicule. The pompous and solemn parade of the priesthood, marching with great dignity around this walled city, with crooked rams' horns in their hands, and exhausting the whole force of their lungs with an expectation, that by this puffing effort they should be able to throw down the stony walls of a city, has something in it of a laughable nature; but the conclusion of the story, if it had any truth in it, would be to a correct mind productive of distress, since indiscriminate and unrelenting murder forms the painful picture. The story of the witch of Endor is too contemptible for serious remark; but when coupled with Lot's wife and with Sampson, the pillar of salt, and the wonderful strength in Sampson's hair, it might serve to frighten children and amuse fools; but to sedate minds, attached to nature and truth, such incoherent stuff must become an object of the highest contempt; the bare mention of such extravagant vagaries ought to be their open refutation. The laws of nature are permanent. God is immutable and truth is immortal. To these great objects the energy of intellect ought to be directed. It is time, therefore, to proceed to the examination of arguments, which the most respectable and enlightened believers in Christianity have deemed sufficient to establish its divine origin. These arguments shall be taken up and stated in their full force, that in this respect Christians shall have no right to complain; the success attending an effort to confute them, must be judged of by the result and mode of execution. It is sufficient that a sincere desire to discover truth will be a constant concomitant of those inquiries.

CHAPTER IX

Is the Evidence Drawn from Miracles Sufficient to Prove the Divine Origin of the Christian Religion?

The sun rises in the eastern horizon with all its resplendent beauties and divine energies, and yet carries along
with it no terror or disorder, no trouble or uneasiness in the
mind of man. Its motion is known to be regulated by a constancy of impulse; by a cause, whose nature and power are
invariable and uniform; by a cause, in which man reposes
the utmost confidence. The stars glisten in the firmament,
unshaken in their position; the moon performs her wonted
duty in the planetary world; in other words, the solar system is guided by laws, of which mathematical science has
taken the most indubitable cognizance. The productions
of earth are subject to no supernatural derangement; they
are exhibited with a constancy and specific similarity which
discard every idea of perversion in physical law, and present the material world as a theatre of certitude which the
efforts of superstition cannot destroy. The tides ebb and flow,
and all the relative operations of nature are preserved entire,

in despite of the malignity of superstition. This vast whole, this extensive universe, thus subjected to the operation of immutable laws, is, nevertheless, distorted and deranged by Christian theology; its Author is insulted, and the scientific deductions of human intellect perverted or destroyed. Religion, not content with the consistency and harmony of Nature, has sought for redress in the violation of her laws, and nothing short of miracles could satisfy the extravagant desires of "pious and holy fanaticism." Pride and vanity have tempted man to establish religion upon a supernatural basis. The idea of associating with heaven, and holding an intercourse with celestial powers, was a circumstance of extravagant and delicious enjoyment, with a privileged order, and laid the foundation of that terrifying severity of judgment contained in the gospel declaration, "He that believeth not shall be damned."

If supernatural religion were a thing founded in truth, it would not seek for so many divers means of support, but would rest itself upon the decisions of human judgments and the general science of the world. A true system of ethics disclaims all foreign aid, all violation of Nature's laws, and stands upon its own intrinsic merit. Miracles make it neither better nor worse; if it be false, miracles cannot make it true, and if it be true in its own nature, the working of miracles cannot make it more true. There cannot, therefore, be any use in miracles, since they do not alter the nature of things, or destroy the force and extent of evidence.

The evidence deduced from the supposed existence of miracles is considered by Christian believers incontrovertible, in regard to the sacred truths in their religion. It is astonishing, say they, that any man can have the audacity to call in question the truth of this system, whose divinity has been proved by the working of so many miracles. Both under the Jewish and Christian dispensations, God manifested his power, and displayed his eternal perfections in support of the holy nature and celestial origin of revealed religion; he stopped the course of the sun, parted the seas, and dried up the rivers, that his chosen people might pass through with safety upon dry land. He raised the dead in the presence of vast multitudes, whose testimony has descended down to us, with undiminished weight and convincing energy. "He has arrested in turn all the powerful laws of nature, in consequence of which, he has established, in the face of the world, the divine origin of the Christian religion. It is, therefore, something worse than folly, it is blindness and madness, mingled with the grossest effrontery to the majesty of Heaven, even to suspect the holy truths of this holy and supernatural system. All that "may" be true; but of its truth we shall be better able to judge when we have thoroughly investigated the subject. Assertions cannot be substituted for arguments, and we have yet to learn whether the weight of evidence drawn from miracles be as great as Christian believers represent. A miracle is a violation of the laws of nature, by "supernatural power." In the act of such violation there must have been some great object in view, which could not otherwise be accomplished; the violation therefore must have been considered as the least of two evils, and the result as productive, upon the whole, of the greatest possible good. But this represents an omnipotent God, surrounded with difficulties, and like imperfect creatures, disposed to make the best of a bad situation.

It will be necessary for those who advocate the doctrine

of miracles, to recur to the cause and primary establishment of the laws of nature. God is infinite in all his perfections; the laws of nature are an effect of the divine attributes, and must have been modified in the best possible manner, and to answer the best and wisest purposes. To alter, therefore, that which already had been done in the best possible manner, would be to make it worse, for no alteration or amendment could make that better which was already as good as it could be. If the world and the laws by which the world was governed, are the offspring of infinite wisdom, they must have been right in the first place, for it is a necessary character of infinite wisdom, to perform whatever it does perform in the best possible manner. All alterations or violations in any system or set of laws, argues imperfection and want of discernment; but such imperfection and want of discernment cannot be the property of a perfect being. If God, therefore, is perfect, such perfection would enable him to conceive and execute with a masterly hand. The mechanic who builds a machine, frequently alters his plan, and is under the necessity of attending to amendments and repairs; but his ignorance was the ground work of this, and a competent knowledge of the principles by which the machine was constructed, would have precluded the necessity of subsequent correction and amendment. The Creator of the world knew perfectly well the force and effect of principle before it was applied to the accomplishment of the variegated motions and operations of existence; ignorance, therefore, could have no share in modifying the vast powers of the universe, or the immutable principles by which it is directed. Wisdom, power, and goodness, combined in the management of the whole, and consequently the whole is formed exactly in such a manner as these three leading perfections of the divine character at first intended. To work a miracle, therefore, would answer no very valuable purpose, and is derogatory to the attributes of God, by which it is supposed to be wrought. To establish a system of religion by evidence drawn from miracles, is to establish it upon the ruin of the consistent harmony of the divine perfections; upon the ruin of all principle and all confidence. When the consistent character of the author of such religion is destroyed, the religion itself is not worth much. Either God did things in the first place as they ought to be done, or he did not; if he did them as they ought be done, there could have been no need of alteration, and consequently there could have been no such thing as a miracle; if he did not, then he must have been either imperfect, or have acted inconsistent with good principle; in either of which cases, his character as God would be destroyed, and the perfection of his existence sacrificed upon the alter of human folly. Fanaticism, which attempts to exalt its God by making him work wonders, is as great an enemy to true Theism, as the open and professed Atheist. A wonder-working God, who violates his own laws, and acts inconsistently with the principles which he himself has established, is no God at all. It is an immoral phantom conjured up in the wild vagaries of superstitious imagination. It is easy to perceive that if there be in nature a perfect God, he cannot be the author of those marvelous and even ridiculous violations of the laws of nature detailed in the Old and New Testament. His character must be uniform, consistent and perfect, just and equitable, and in perfect coincidence with the immortal laws of the moral and physical world.

All things, it is said, are possible with God. This is one of the maxims of that religion which has perverted all the principles of truth and justice; but this maxim is not true, it is not possible, for instance, that God should destroy his own existence; it is not possible that he should act inconsistently with the properties and principles of his nature. This extravagant assertion, instead of exalting the character of the Creator, would absolutely destroy it, by causing him to act without rule and without justice. But superstition can never do enough for her God, until she has done a great deal too much. A consistent and immutable Deity, acting in strict conformity to the essential properties of his existence, would be, in the estimation of inconsistent superstition, an object far inferior to those wild and unruly divinities, who overturn states and empires, pervert the general order of nature, and occasionally, by way of amusement, drown the whole world, with all the inhabitants and animals therein existing. A man walking regularly upon the earth, and performing with fidelity all his moral duties, "is by no means an object of attachment," but one walking upon the water, without doing any good, will draw forth the admiration of a gazing, foolish, and superstitious world. The passion for the marvelous has carried man from earth to heaven; and, in the ranting fury of his zeal, he has supposed that his God would be pleased with all those moral distortions which at such unhappy moments agitated his own delirious mind. The idea of the existence of a miracle will be wholly destroyed by a just recurrence to the counter-balancing evidence, drawn from the experience of mankind. This experience bears testimony to the uniform operation of Nature's laws; it teaches man to repose in them unqualified confidence, and, in all the common concerns of life, this confidence serves as the foundation of his courage, his activity, and his consolation. Here are, then, two kinds of evidence opposed to each other; the one human experience, and the other human testimony.

Those who contend that miracles prove the divinity of the Christian religion, appeal to the testimony of witnesses to support the truth and existence of such miracles. Let this case be examined, and the superior weight of evidence will appear with convincing force. Believers declare that the miracles which were wrought to prove the truth of the holy Scriptures, were numerous, and performed before great numbers of people. That the credit and veracity of these witnesses cannot be doubted; that they were honest and disinterested men; that they did not wish to be deceived themselves, nor could they possibly reap any advantage from deceiving others; that some of the eye witnesses were inspired men, in whom there was no guile, and that others were mere men of the world, whose feelings and interest would have rejected, if possible, the splendour of such supernatural evidence; that all these, however, yielded to the mighty energy of the mighty God; that they pronounced him a wonder-working God, and that such marvelous facts had never before been presented to a wicked and apostate world. It is also declared and maintained, that the result of these pure and incorruptible witnesses has been transmitted down for more than two thousand years through the holy and incorruptible channel of the Church of Christ; that the present generation might as well doubt of the existence of Scipio or of Caesar, as to doubt of the existence of Jesus Christ and his apostles, and the miracles which by them were performed; that the unbeliever at this time is working against all his own positions, destroying the nature of evidence, and unhinging the moral world.

Formidable as this statement may appear, it will perhaps vanish when compared with the weight of evidence drawn from the almost universal experience of the human race. The laws of nature are uniform and immutable. This is declared to be a fact by the testimony of all ages and all countries. Observation and experience are the sources which must be resorted to in such cases, and these do not warrant a conclusion that the laws of nature have ever been violated. Through a long succession of ages, the same general facts and events have been presented; the same causes appear to have been in a constant state of action, productive of the same or similar effects, and to the general order of the physical world, every living creature now bears testimony. When, therefore, it is asserted, that in former ages all this beauty and harmony of the world was destroyed, this ought not to overbalance the convincing force of evidence drawn from our own observations. If we say that we believe the former extravagant accounts, we contradict the testimony of our own senses; we abandon the instructive guide of our own experience, and affirm that the testimony of a few men has more weight than our own positive knowledge.

The human mind is bound to decide according to the greatest portion of evidence; in any given case, therefore, the nature and portion of evidence ought to be fairly called up before the mind, and perspicuity of statement, will probably induce the necessity of a favourable and upright decision. Will any Christian believer say that he has as much evidence that nature's laws have been violated, or that miracles have been wrought, as he has that the laws of nature have not been violated, and that no miracles have been wrought? Certainly the testimony of a few men bears no proportion to the universal experience and general observation of the human species. All mankind, with a few exceptions, declare that the world is governed by laws which do not change. A few men who lived many ages ago, declared that these laws did change, and that they had been witnesses to several astonishing facts of this kind. If we give credit to those men, we give the lie to all the world beside; if we repose confidence in the testimony of our own senses, and the general experience of mankind, we shall have reason to believe, that those few men, who relate prodigies and miracles, were either deceived themselves, or that they had a design to deceive others. It is not extraordinary for ignorant men, or even the most scientific, to be frequently deceived; nor is it at all extraordinary, that either the ignorant or the learned should form a settled plan for deceiving their fellow creatures. Either of these cases is much more probable than that God should violate his own laws, or act contrary to the essential properties of his existence. Either of these cases is much more probable, than that the experience and observation of all mankind, in almost all ages, should have been incorrect or incapable of judging upon so plain a case as the operation of the laws of nature. Men are frequently interested in the practice of deception, or at least they conceive that a temporary advantage would be the result; they therefore yield to an impulse productive of misery in the end, but calculated to gratify for the moment the extravagant and vicious inclinations of the individual. Men are sometimes disposed to tell lies, but nature speaks the language of solemn truth. To controvert, therefore, this truth, and adhere to the stories of a few fanatic and ignorant individuals, is the height of folly. In no other case is man so unwise; in no other case does he so essentially depart from the rules of evidence and the respect which he owes to the dignity of his intellectual existence.

Further considerations of corroborative weight and influence will be found essentially connected with the nature of

this subject, by a recurrence to the history of intellectual existence, and the state of improvement in society. It is extraordinary, that all miracles have been wrought during the dark
ages; and that a cultivated state of human existence has always
excluded and rejected all such marvelous events. The smallest attention that has been paid to the historical progress of
science, will convince us that there are most wonders where
there is most ignorance. That knowledge has been always
unfriendly to the existence of miracles; that ghosts, witches,
and devils, with all their concomitant train of mischievous
and malignant phantoms, have generally existed amidst the
darkness, the ignorance, and the superstition of former ages;
and that in proportion as science advanced, miracle receded;
in proportion as knowledge was generally diffused, the marvelous stories of antiquity became less respectable, and their
supposed truth more universally doubted. There was a time,
and that not very far distant, in which the foolish story of the
witch of Endor was received with the greatest respect; at this
moment, enlightened Christians themselves are ashamed of
it. In proportion as man makes progress in physical knowledge, he ceases to be the dupe of superstition, and what before
appeared marvelous, now becomes plain and intelligible. In
natural philosophy we may discover a hundred proofs of the
truth of this assertion; the rapid lightning of Heaven, which
darts with inconceivable velocity through the regions of space,
was once considered as a powerful weapon of destruction in
the hands of God, and that no human power could control
it. This modification of physical energy, among enlightened
minds, has lost all its terror, and in many places is completely
subjected to the will of man. The cause of earthquakes is
known, and scientific presumption has gone so far as to make
even those that are artificial. The charms and deceptions of

legerdemain tricks have lost, in a high degree, their influence, and strength of intellect is determined to oppose with constancy and firmness such impositions upon the human race.

If there were no other circumstance which operated against miracles, the ignorance, with which believers applaud them, would, of itself, be a sufficient condemnation and refutation of such idle and foolish stories. The witches of antiquity have fled to the mountains; the prophets are no longer credited, and the possibility of miracles is not admitted by the mathematical and physical reason.

If miracles ever had any existence, why should they not have an existence still? There is as much reason for them now as there ever was, and the necessity is increased by the infidelity of the present day. If miracles were necessary to establish Christianity in the first instance, they are equally proper and necessary now; for proofs ought to be equal to all, where equal credence is demanded. To make the Christian religion consistent, it is necessary there should be a constant string of miracles in every age and in all countries; but this would destroy the very nature of miracles, by making them so frequent, that it would be impossible to distinguish between these events, and those which were produced by the common operations of Nature. It is, therefore, impossible to give equal proof to all those who are equally interested in the ultimate decision upon revealed religion.

Every supernatural system has pretended to miracles, to something mysterious and marvelous, to something out of the order of Nature, and which would be calculated to excite alarm amongst weak and ignorant people. The truth is, there can be no such thing as a miracle, and the religion that is built upon this foundation is false, and cannot be permanent. The laws of Nature are immutable, and God, their author, is free from every species of imperfection. Truth, immortality, and eternal uniformity of action, are essential to his character and existence. The evidence drawn from universal experience is against the possibility of a miracle, and the history of mankind corroborates the impressive opinion, that the moral and physical world is governed by laws "inherent in the nature of things, identified with their existence," and incapable of being altered by the properties or exertion of any being whatever. Christian believers assert that their system is the only one supported by miracles; but they ought to know that Mahomet lays equal claim to the working of miracles, has declared that he traveled through ninety heavens in one night, and returned to Mecca, in Arabia, before the next morning. That he saw God Almighty, and held with him a personal conversation, together with many other strange things of a miraculous and terrifying nature. There is as much reason to believe Mahomet as to believe Moses and Jesus, and their apostles and followers.

The fact is, there is no reason to believe any of them, unless the stories which they relate are consistent with the nature of things, and the character of God. All deviations from this divine standard are to be suspected of error; and miracles most of all. It is extraordinary that Jesus, who is said to have wrought so many miracles, was afterwards put to death in the very place where they were wrought, and by the very persons who had been eye witnesses of such divine and supernatural power. "If the Jews demanded the death of Jesus, his miracles are at once annihilated in the mind of every rational man." It cannot be presumed, that a man clothed with supernatural power, would be a proper object of execution, in the estimation of those who really believed that he was in the possession and exercise of such power, and that all his efforts were aided and sanctioned by the Creator himself. If the proofs of this celestial mission of Jesus had been clearly exhibited through the channel of miraculous operations, the Jews and all the surrounding multitude would have adored him as a God, and they would have been terrified at the very idea of laying violent hands upon one whose omnipotence could have instantly crushed them to atoms. The following remarks upon this subject, taken from a powerful reasoner, deserve to be inserted here:

"To suppose that God can alter the settled laws of Nature, which he himself formed, is to suppose his will and wisdom mutable, and that they are not the best laws of the most perfect being; for if he is the author of them, they must be immutable as he is; so that he cannot alter them to make them better, and will not alter them to make them worse. Neither of these can be agreeable to his attributes. If the course of nature is not the best, the only best and fittest that could be, it is not the offspring of perfect wisdom, nor was it settled by divine will; and then God is not the author of nature, if the laws thereof can be altered; for if the laws of nature are God's laws, he cannot alter them in any degree, without being in some degree changeable. If all nature is under the direction of an immutable mind, what can make a change in that direction? God must be allowed to be eternal, therefore he necessarily exists, and is necessarily whatever he is; therefore it is not in his own power to change himself; it is his perfection to be immutable; for if his nature could possibly change, it might err; for whosoever is changeable is not perfect. Beside, an eternal and a perfect nature must necessarily be unchangeable; and as long as the first moving cause is the same, all subsequent and second causes can never vary."

This reasoning is energetic and conclusive against the doctrine of miracles. If, then, there can be no such thing as a miracle, Christianity, which is built upon this foundation, must also be false. Man must therefore resort to a system of morality and religion which coincides with the laws of nature, and which discards all supernatural violation of its divine order and harmony.

CHAPTER X

Prophetic Evidence in Relation to the Divinity of the Christian Religion

The fulfillment of the prophecies is considered by Christian believers, as strong proof of the sacred and celestial nature of their religion. They speak in language positive, and in confidence bold and firm, that the divinity of that holy system, which they believe, is substantiated by many wonders, and that they have a surplus of evidence in favor of its "holy truths." Miracles, although sufficient of themselves to prove that revealed religion is true, are corroborated by the convincing evidence drawn from predictive declaration contained in the scriptures. Many centuries ago, and even thousands of years, the favorites of heaven were inspired with a clear and certain knowledge of important events, which subsequent times should disclose to the human race. The predictions of these men have been literally fulfilled, and this circumstance of itself ought to be sufficient to destroy the infidelity of the present age. This idea is considered by Christians as founded in truth, and they challenge a confutation of its force and effect. It is therefore necessary that we inquire whether this species of evidence can have weight in the present case. Prophecy is in some respects like miracles, they both partake of the marvelous, they are both supernatural, they are both inconsistent with the order of nature. There is, however, in man, a pride and vanity which induces him to pretend to a knowledge of futurity, and that his knowledge is the result of a secret and mysterious intercourse with celestial powers. In all ages there have been prophets who imposed upon the mass of mankind, and made others believe that the events of future ages were opened to their view. It is not extraordinary that such men should have existed, nor is it extraordinary that many of the human race should have reposed a confidence in them. Ignorance is the cause of credulity, and it is with ignorance that imposture always works, but it is extraordinary that learned men have cited the scripture prophecies in proof of their religion, as will appear more fully when the objections to which these prophecies are exposed, are fully disclosed and examined. The argument which goes to destroy the nature of a miracle, equally destroys the possibility of man's possessing from God a prophetic spirit; it is a violation of the laws of nature, a derangement of its natural and regular course, an infringement of the correct operation of the moral and mental faculties of our existence. But there are two grand objections which lie against scripture prophecies, and which must destroy all their credit and authority. The first is, that they are so vague and indefinite, that they cannot be applied to any specific object, person, or event. The second is, that those which are the most clear and explicit, have absolutely failed in their accomplishment, and this of itself is sufficient to overturn the divinity of any book in which such prophecies are to be found. A third consideration of weight, is the deception and lying character of the Bible prophets, and even God himself is blasphemously charged of having a hand in this wicked business, by putting a lying spirit into the mouth of one of his prophets. (See 2d Chron. chapter 18.)

If the business of prophesying were admissible in any shape, it is that only which includes the perspicuity and certainty of time, place, person, object, and circumstance. There can be no use in prophesying, if nobody can tell to what object it is directed, and what is its real and true meaning. A prophecy that may be applied to twenty different objects, is no prophecy at all; or at least there would be no occasion for a divine spirit in such predictions. It ought to be called conjecture or mere "guess work," for any man might prophesy after this manner; if it did not suit one thing, it would perhaps another, and in the multitude of events that are constantly disclosed, it would be strange indeed if there was not some event to which the prophecy would in some measure apply. Fanaticism would then step in to aid the application, and a few councils, synods, and presbyteries, by the force of zeal and authority, could easily place the matter beyond the confutation of all the infidels of the world; at any rate, they could declare that if any man did not believe that the prophecy meant exactly what they said it meant, "he should be damned." This, if it did not make the prediction clear, would at least make the church strong, and in its authority henceforth infallible.

It is pretended that the coming and second coming of Jesus Christ is clearly predicted in the "sacred books" of the Jews and Christians; but those predictions in the Old Testament, which divines so dexterously apply to the Advent of the Son of Mary, are as applicable to any other person as they are to Jesus. It is sufficient in this place, to notice two or three

passages which have always been prominent in the estimation
of believers upon this subject. "The sceptre shall not depart
from Judah, nor a lawgiver from between his feet, until Shiloh
come." This, it is said, has an immediate reference to the first
appearance of the Savior of the world; but admitting that the
prophecy was correct in point of time, it is deficient in designation of person. It is impossible to tell who "Shiloh" is, and
it would apply as well to Mahomet as to Jesus. The Christians
assert that this prophecy was fulfilled; but the Jews, who ought
to understand their own sacred writings better than the followers of Jesus, declare that it has not been fulfilled. If, however,
the passage really had reference to the coming of Christ, why
did it not express, in plain terms that could not have been mis-
taken, its real meaning, together with the name of the person,
the place where he was born, and the time and place when and
where he was executed, and by whom. This would have put the
matter beyond controversy; the designation of Jesus by name,
the name of his mother, and the peculiar circumstance of his
death, would have been much better calculated to silence the
objections of individuals, and prophecy would have become
much more respectable in the view of reason. The seed of the
woman shall bruise the serpent's head, is another prophecy
which Christians declare relates immediately to their Savior.
But it is impossible to discover any specific application of such
a vague and indefinite assertion as this. The plainest explanation that can be given to the phrase is, that men, being the
offspring of women, should find in themselves a disposition to
bruise the heads of serpents, wherever they could find them;
but what has this to do with religion or the coming of Jesus
Christ? If the passage has any meaning of this latter kind, the
words are not calculated to disclose such meaning, and we
are just as ignorant as if it had never been spoken.

In the 7th chapter of Isaiah, there is another famous prophecy in the following words: "Behold a Virgin shall conceive and bear a son, and shall call his name Emanuel. Butter and honey shall he eat, that he may know to refuse the evil, and choose the good." This prophecy declares that at some future time, some girl or other should be with child, and that the child's name should be called Emanuel; this is the whole amount of it, and it is easy to perceive that it is remarkably deficient in all definite properties of perspicuous prediction. The name of Mary is not mentioned, nor the name of Jesus; nobody knows who this virgin was, or by whom she became pregnant; all that is pointed and specific in this prophecy is the name of the child, and this is Emanuel, and not Jesus. The son of Mary, therefore, whom the Christians have exalted to be the Savior of a wicked world, is not included within the meaning of this prophecy; or at least, if they meant that the prophecy should apply to Christ, it is a pity that they had not called him by name, and pointed out the time and place of his birth. This would have prevented much doubt and difficulty, and been more consistent with the perfections of that God who is bound to instruct and not deceive his creatures. There is one further observation upon the nature of this prophetic passage, which is, that after declaring that Emanuel should eat butter and honey, and the reason that is offered for this, is, that he might know how to refuse the evil and choose the good; as if the way to discriminate with correctness between moral and immoral principles, was to live upon butter and honey.

It is probably true that such a mode of living rendered habitual would be favorable to the moral temperament of man, and that the use of animal food makes him savage and ferocious. It ought not, however, to have been mentioned as a principal cause of distinguishing between good and evil. This is the work of the moral and mental faculties of our existence, and some men might eat honey during their whole lives, and die at last totally ignorant of moral principle. This passage of holy writ, in its real nature and character, does not deserve the least comment or observation; but when Christian theology has made mole hills into mountains, it is a duty which we owe to the cause of truth, to strip the film from off the eye, that nature may appear correct and without distortion. When prophecies are expressed in such a loose and unmeaning manner, they lose all their character and credit, and can never be cited as proof of the divinity of that religion in which they are found.

Whoever wishes to be more fully convinced, that scripture prophecies are destitute of all certitude, is referred to the perusal of a work, entitled, "Christianity as old as the Creation," in which numerous passages of this kind are called up to view, and the reader is furnished with chapter and verse in various places of the Old and New Testament. In the second place, that prophecies do not prove the truth of the Christian religion, is evident from the consideration, that some of those which are most clear and explicit, have absolutely failed in their accomplishment. The twenty-fourth chapter of Matthew is adduced to prove the present assertion; in that chapter Christ foretelleth the destruction of Jerusalem, and the end of the world; the inquiry being made, when shall these things be accomplished, the answer is, that this generation shall not pass away till all these things be fulfilled. But it is necessary to quote the whole passage, to show that this prophecy, which is as clear and definite as any one contained either in the Old or New Testament, has not been fulfilled; that the

time of its fulfillment expired long ago, even in that generation in which it was spoken, and that this of itself ought to
destroy the validity of all Christian prophecies; because, when
detected in one positive and absolute falsehood, the veracity
of Testament writers is for ever afterwards to be suspected.
(Ver. 29th) "Immediately after the tribulation of those days,
shall the sun be darkened, and the moon shall not give her
light, and the stars shall fall from heaven, and the powers of
the heavens shall be shaken. And then shall appear the sign
of the son of man in heaven; and then shall all the tribes of
the earth mourn, and they shall see the son of man coming in
the clouds of heaven with power and great glory; and he shall
send his angels with a great sound of a trumpet, and they shall
gather together his elect from the four winds, from one end
of heaven to the other. Now learn the parable of the fig tree;
when his branches are yet tender, and putteth forth leaves, ye
know that summer is nigh; so likewise ye, when ye shall see
all these things, know that it is near, even at the doors. Verily I say unto you, this generation shall not pass till all these
things be fulfilled. Heaven and earth shall pass away, but my
word shall not pass away."

The things predicted in this passage have not come to pass.
The sun has not been darkened, nor has the moon ceased to
give her light; the stars still shine in brilliant splendor, they
glisten in the expansive firmament, they still hold their sta-
tionary predicament in the regions of space, and are expressive
of the majestic grandeur and resplendent glory of the Creator.
There is no Christian that can contend that this prophecy has
been fulfilled; every thing contained in it was to have taken
place before that generation should pass away; but not only
that generation, but many others have passed away; eighteen

hundred years have elapsed, and the things spoken of are not yet accomplished; there is a complete failure, the prophecy is false, and this falsifies the book in which it is contained. A single detection of this kind is enough to destroy the credit and authority, the pretended divinity and celestial origin of the New Testament. If God the Creator had inspired the men who wrote it, they would have written nothing but truth, for it is impossible that he should have inspired them with lies. There are many other places in the New Testament which speak of the day of judgment, and the final termination of the world, as if it were expected that those events would actually have taken place during the life-time of the apostles or immediate followers of Jesus. (See Cor. x. 11., Heb. ix. 21., I John ii. 18.) If those men who pretended to be inspired, were nevertheless so grossly deceived, what confidence can the human race now repose in their writings? It is evident that the end of the world was expected as an event that must shortly happen, and that the apostles waited for it with trembling anxiety, frequently impressing on each other the importance of being prepared for the opening of such a terrific scene.

Nature, which is constant, stable, and uniform, has given lie to all these predictions, and taught man a lesson of impressive science, that God is just, immutable, and eternal; that he regards with parental benevolence the creation which he has made, and that he will not wantonly destroy it to gratify the imaginary whims of a blind and bigoted fanaticism. But there is still a more weighty charge, a more important accusation lying against the Bible prophecies. They charge the Creator of the world with a want of veracity; that one part of his business has been to deceive his own prophets, and to infuse into their minds falsehood and lies. The Bible represents him as co-partner in human guilt, and exhibiting on many occasions a departure from the rules of moral excellence, which departure in itself would be derogatory to the character of any individual of the human race. In the 2d Chronicles, chapter xviii. we shall find matter to verify what has been said. The passage is as follows: "And the Lord said, who shall entice Ahab king of Israel, that he may go up and fall at Ramoth Gilead? And one spake saying after this manner. Then there came out a spirit and stood before the Lord, and said, I will entice him, and the Lord said unto him, wherewith? And he said, I will go out and be a lying spirit in the mouth of all his prophets. And the Lord said, thou shalt entice him, and thou shalt also prevail; go out and do even so. Now, therefore, behold the Lord hath put a lying spirit in the mouth of these thy prophets, and the Lord hath spoken evil against thee." Here God is positively charged with having put a lying spirit into the mouth of his prophet, and this, if true, would completely destroy his moral character; if it be not true, the assertion in the Bible is false, and of course destroys the divine authenticity of the book. In either alternative, the believer is involved in equal difficulty; the truth of the book or the character of God must be sacrificed. Another example of this kind of prophesying, is found in the 18th chapter of Deuteronomy. "When a prophet speaketh in the name of the Lord, if the thing follow not, nor come to pass, that is the thing which the Lord has not spoken, but the prophet hath spoken it presumptuously, thou shalt not be afraid of him." The prophet Jeremiah says, "O Lord, thou hast deceived me, and I was deceived; thou are stronger than I, and hast prevailed. Wilt thou be altogether unto me as a liar, and as waters that fail?" And in another prophet, the Lord says, "the days are prolonged and every vision fails;" and though the

Lord adds, "thus shall none of my words be prolonged any more, but the word which I have spoken shall be done;" yet he afterwards says, if the prophet be deceived when he hath spoken a thing, "I the Lord have deceived that prophet." And if the prophet is deceived, must not the people who rely on that prophet be deceived? And does not the prophet Jeremiah say, "Ah! Lord God, surely thou hast greatly deceived this people!" (See Tindal, page 220.)

It is not the intention, nor is it necessary in a work of this kind, to examine all the pages of the sacred writings of the Christians, in proof of their falsehood or immorality; a few specimens are sufficient to substantiate the principle which is placed in opposition to the character and doctrine of revealed religion. God cannot lie; he is incapable of deception, and a book which charges him with these crimes is false upon the very face of the record. This charge which has been exhibited in the quotations which are made above, furnishes a strong ground of belief, that those who wrote the scriptures were unacquainted with the nature of moral principles, and that they had no correct idea of the nature of Theism. Lying prophets, a lying book, and a God that coincides with such detestable principles, are circumstances irreconcilable, inconsistent, unjust, and destitute of all truth. A prophet who tells lies himself, and then attributes these lies to the Creator of the world, is a character which reason ought to abhor. This impious connection between earth and heaven; this pretended combination for the purposes of fraud and deception, is calculated only to disgust an innocent mind, and produce an implacable hatred against all religion. It would be more consistent with the true interest of man, that he should be destitute of all theological ideas, than that he should yield to the reception of such incoherent and unjust opinions of the divine character. Atheism is far preferable to that theology which includes folly, cruelty, and ferocious fanaticism. A God that inspires people with lies is worse than no God at all, and such is the character of the Bible God, if the passages of scripture cited above are to be credited. Prophecy has nothing to do with the order of nature, it is not in conformity to it, it is a wild and injurious effect of the most extravagant superstition. It appears from the preceding inquiry, that many of the scripture prophecies are vague and indefinite, that they prove nothing in regard to the supernatural origin of revealed religion; in other cases, the prophetic spirit has not hit the mark, and the prophecy has completely failed of accomplishment; in others, the lies and deception incorporated with these celestial predictions, annihilate at once all the vestiges of truth, and leave the moral world in a state of mental decrepitude, ignorance, and superstition. To assert, therefore, that the evidence drawn from prophecies is sufficient to substantiate the divinity of the Christian religion is a complete abandonment of all the laws and principles by which nature is governed. It is a surrender of intellect to the capricious and extravagant operations of a cruel and superstitious opinion. It is substituting conjecture for truth, and making the imagination more correct and powerful than reason. It is not possible that the intellectual powers of human nature can ever reach an exalted state of improvement, till they rise above all the degrading impressions of theological superstition, and rest with confidence upon the basis of their own energy.

CHAPTER XI

That the Immorality of the Christian Religion Proves that it is Not of Divine Origin

It is extraordinary that, among other sources of evidence to which Christians have resorted for the purpose of proving their religion divine and supernatural, they have yielded to a belief that in point of moral excellence the Bible is superior to all other books. If all external evidence were swept away, it would, nevertheless, appear by the internal purity of this system that it is divine. Its morality is declared to be pure, excellent, and celestial; that it rises above the earth, and partakes of the nature of heaven, that its maxims are sublime, its doctrines holy, its moral precepts universally unexceptionable, and that the mind that does not perceive in the Christian religion indubitable marks of its divinity, must be blind to that blaze of internal evidence which shines with refulgent splendour through this revealed system. Such in substance is the opinion, such the sentiments and feelings of the Christian believer. It is certainly of the highest importance, that every system of religion should be immaculate in its moral principles; and in deficiency of this, its pretended claim to divinity sinks into nothing, and merits absolute contempt. All the miracles in the world can never prove that religion to be true, whose internal maxims are immoral and destructive. Purity of rules and principles, must be fundamental in every ethical treatise; that nature of our existence demands it, our powers bear a constant relation to the production of moral effects, and our happiness cannot be secured by any other means. A single departure from the pre-eminent principles of an exalted virtue, is sufficient to condemn to everlasting infamy, any pretended supernatural system, in which such departure is discovered. It is expected, in mere human productions, that errors will frequently appear; but in a work that is divine, there can be no excuse for faults of any kind, not even in a single instance. If the Christian religion be the work of a divine and Almighty mind, it should have been presented free from blemish and moral impurity; it should have been clear, intelligible, upright, and immaculate in all its principles; it should have come clothed with innocence, and untarnished by that debauchery and blood, which now constitute so considerable a portion of this "holy" and "divine" system. It is called a system, but in what respect it deserves this appellation, it is impossible to say. It is in conformity to common phraseology that we so frequently include it under this name. It is not systematic either in its history, its doctrines, or its morality; it consists of detached historical anecdotes, false or mutilated moral rules, and unintelligible dogmas. They are bound up together in one book; but they have as little connection with each other, as the history of Greece and the accounts of the Salem witchcraft. In a genuine system of ethics, it is expected, at least, that glaring immorality will be excluded, and that the fundamental principles will coincide with the nature and powers of man. But when we behold in a book the grossest violation of theoretic moral excellence and practical purity, the greatest indecency and the most disgusting indelicacy of sentiment, there is good ground to suspect that such a book has been the production of weak and vicious men, and not the work of infinite wisdom. It is, however, denied by Christians, that their religion contains maxims and principles of an immoral nature; it is therefore necessary to furnish incontrovertible proofs of this position, and show in what respects the Bible is at war with moral virtue, the peace of society, and the best interests of man. It is necessary to show that this book contains maxims and commands which are said to have come from God, which would disgrace the character of any honest man, and make him a candidate for a state prison or the gallows.

When the chosen people of God were about to leave the land of Egypt, he commanded them to borrow from the Egyptians, jewels of silver, and jewels of gold, without any intention of ever returning them to their proper owners, but to march off and appropriate them exclusively to their own use. Here was deception, and a breach of trust of so black a complexion, that it was very little better than downright theft or open plunder. Of a similar nature is the conduct of Jesus, when he sent his disciples to bring him a colt that was none of his own. In case of a detection or attack, he ordered his disciples to answer, that the Lord had need of him. Such a trifling evasion at the present day would not be considered as a valid excuse for feloniously taking and carrying away anther man's property. If it was right at that time to steal in the name of the Lord, or get clear of the crime, by saying that the Lord had need of the stolen goods, it is right yet, and such a maxim once admitted would overturn the empire of justice, and subvert the order and peace of society. There are many heavy crimes and high handed misdemeanors, which lie very strong against the chosen people of God; and if the accounts of immorality detailed in the Old Testament, concerning the Jews, are true, we should be led to conclude that God had not made a very wise choice. The history of that barbarous people, is the history of carnage and murder, of theft, robbery, and almost every species of villainy, that ever disgraced an ignorant and savage nation. It is to be presumed, that if God would condescend to become partial to any of the human race, and make them his chosen people, he would choose those that were already strongly attached to the practice of an exalted virtue, or that he would instantly instruct them in the knowledge of useful, moral, and sublime principles. This, however, is not the fact of the present case; the Jews knew nothing of morality or science, before God made them his chosen people, and they knew nothing of it afterward; so that their intimacy with their God was of no advantage to "them," and still less to their "neighbors." To their neighbors it was the sword of vengeance and slaughter; for when they were impelled to the abominable crimes of unrelenting murder and universal pillage, they charge it upon God, and said, for so doing, they had his immediate command. In proof of this, various passages might be cited; but a few are sufficient to destroy the credit of the Bible, and free the divine character from such odious imputations. In the 20th chapter of Deuteronomy, the following bloody and exterminating commands are given, and these commands are attributed to God himself, (Verse 13th) "And when the Lord thy God hath delivered it into thine hands, thou shalt smite every male thereof with the edge of the sword. But the women and little ones, and the cattle, and all that is in the city, even all the spoil thereof shalt thou take unto thyself." (Verse 16th) "But of the cities of these people, which the Lord thy God doth give thee for an inheritance, thou shalt save alive nothing that breatheth. But thou shalt utterly destroy them." In the sixth chapter of Joshua, there is another specimen of the immoral and murdering spirit of God's chosen people. (Verse 21) "And they utterly destroyed all that was in the city, both man and woman, young and old, and ox, and sheep, and ass, with the edge of the sword." To charge the Creator of the world with such a violation of all justice, with such a dereliction of every humane sentiment, is to deprive him of all his moral perfections, and to make him equal in villainy to Moses and Joshua, or any of the eminent murderers whose names have been recorded in the bloody history of the human race. It is strange to observe, that in reasoning upon theological subjects, men are disposed to abandon the correct ground of moral decision, and contend that those actions which would be unjust in man, would nevertheless be just when performed by the Creator. This is a mode of reasoning that perverts all the faculties of our existence, destroys the moral excellence of Deity, and overturns the foundation of principle. In all beings that are intelligent, moral principle is the same; and God has no more right to violate it, than any other being. He is essentially bound by the properties of his existence, and his character cannot be sustained without an undeviating attention to the immutable principle of justice.

In the history of David and Solomon, there is such a flagrant violation of justice and decency, that the character of these men is most certainly incompatible with the idea of celestial association. David, who is said to be a man after God's own heart, was, nevertheless, a murderer and adulterer. Solomon, though declared by Christians to be the wisest man, was, probably, one of the most debauched characters that ever disgraced the annals of human history. The chapters in which his love intrigues are celebrated, are an extravagant specimen of the most sensual and lascivious enjoyment. It is impossible to read at the head of some of the chapters, "Christ's love to the Church," without smiling at theological stupidity, or being disgusted with religious deception. There is not a word in all the songs of Solomon, which has the least relation to religion; they are descriptive of sensual love. In some places grossly, and in others delicately touched off by the hand of a descriptive artist. If the Church of Christ at the present day possessed moral sentiment enough to produce a blush, its cheek would be crimsoned over at the idea of incorporating with a system of divinity, this ludicrous and lascivious poem. But fanaticism is blind to the errors and imperfections of any book to which it is determined to be attached. Zeal propels the faculties to discover in nature, debauched or distorted, a real love between Christ and the Church, or a system of morality far superior to every other ethical treatise. This wicked system, which inculcates theft, murder, fornication, and lies, is denominated "holy writ." If such be the character of holy writ, it is far better to seek for moral consolation in productions of another kind. It is a blasphemous application of the terms, and subverts all human confidence in the purity and truth of natural religion. In this religion there is certitude, consistency, and moral virtue. Of all the books that ever were published, Volney's "Ruins" is preeminently entitled to the appellation of "Holy Writ, and ought to be appointed to be read in Churches;" not by his majesty's special command, but by the universal consent and approbation of all those who love nature, truth, and human happiness.

In the New Testament, many principles are advanced

inconsistent with moral truth, destructive of the peace of society, and subversive of the best interests of the human race. Some of these ruinous and immoral sentiments must be noticed, and made the subject of useful comment. "The gospel of Jesus Christ" is announced to a wicked world, as a great and important blessing; but an examination of this system will show that it is calculated to annihilate every thing valuable in human existence; to create endless wars among the nations of the earth; to destroy peace and tranquility; discourage industry, and arrest the energetic progress of the human faculties in their career of beneficial improvement. In proof of these assertions, the following passages are quoted: (Luke chap. xiv. verse 26) "If any man come to me, and hate not his father, and mother, and wife, and children, and brethren, and sisters, yea, and his own life, he cannot be my disciple." In the gospel of St. Matthew we are commanded to love our enemies. By what strange perversion of moral sentiment is it, that we are commanded in one place to hate our nearest relations, and in another to exercise a tender and affectionate regard to our implacable enemies? Such a violation of consistency in a moral code, annihilates at once all human confidence, destroys the finest feelings of the heart, and renders it indubitably certain that such a book cannot be divine or true.

The above passage is also inconsistent with that part of the decalogue which says, "Honor thy father and thy mother;" for surely we cannot hate and honor them at the same time. It is also expressly contradictory to the mild and benevolent temper so frequently exhibited in the Epistles of John. "If any man say that he is in the light and hateth his brother, he is in darkness, even until now." If the above passage in Luke be true, the condition on which we are to become the disciples of Christ, is that of hating our brother, and all our relations; while in the writings of John, love is absolutely necessary to the idea of true religion. How these opposite declarations can stand together, it is difficult to conceive. Christian fanaticism is able, perhaps, to reconcile them; but reason sees in them nothing but inconsistency, and the heated zeal of an incorrect and disordered imagination. Another passage of most destructive immorality, is in Matthew's Gospel (chap. x. verse 35) "Think not that I am come to send peace on earth; I come not to send peace, but a sword. For I am come to set a man at variance against his father, and the daughter against her mother, and the daughter in law against her mother in law, and a man's foes shall be of his own household." If this was really the object of Christ's mission, no man was ever sent upon a more bloody and baneful expedition. This is carrying the sword of war into the hearts of nations, and sowing the seeds of private animosity, in the bosom of domestic life. It is inconsistent with the goodness of God, that he should have been the author of a religion which has annihilated rational peace, and subverted the foundation of social and domestic tranquility. The same dreadful idea is expressed in other parts of the New Testament, and furnishes an immutable ground of decision against the moral principle and divinity of this religion. But not content with spreading far and wide the baleful effects of public and private calamity, this revealed system has positively enjoined, what, if reduced to practice, would bring upon the world universal starvation, and cause the human race to become extinct. (See Matthew chap. vi.) "Therefore I say unto you, take no thought for your life, what ye shall eat or what ye shall drink; nor yet for your body what ye shall put on. Is not the life more than meat, and the body than raiment? Behold the fowls of the air; for they sow not, neither do they reap, nor gather into barns, yet your heavenly Father feedeth them. Are ye not much better than they? Which of you by taking thought, can add one cubit unto his stature? And why take ye thought for raiment? Consider the lilies of the field how they grow; they toil not, neither do they spin; And yet I say unto you that even Solomon in all his glory, was not arrayed like one of these. Therefore take no thought saying, what shall we eat; or what shall we drink, or wherewithal shall we be clothed?" If these directions were followed, the corporeal and mental industry of man would be destroyed, and famine, ignorance, and misery would be the necessary consequence. It is in vain that we are told that these passages do not mean what they express; if, when we are told that we ought to love our enemies, it is meant that we should "not" love them; and when we are told that we ought to hate our nearest relations, it is meant that we should "not" hate them; if when we are told that we ought to take no thought for the morrow, it is meant that we "should" take thought. If such be the explanatory methods by which the injurious force of these passages is to be done away, there is an end to all confidence in language, and the religion of Jesus is better calculated for deception than instruction. The writings of Paul, that heated and fanatic zealot in the Christian faith, are equally noxious to the cause of moral virtue, and are calculated to annihilate the most virtuous efforts of every individual. "It is not of him that willeth nor of him that runneth; not of works lest any man should boast; of ourselves we can do nothing;" together with a hundred other passages of a similar nature, which go directly to suppress all the elevated exertions of the human faculties, and if literally followed, would turn man from intelligent activity, to a state of brutal indolence. It is extremely destructive to the moral happiness of mankind to teach them the want of powers, or the inadequacy of those they possess; because the fact is other-wise, because it is a solemn truth that the powers of man are competent to provide for his happiness; they are equal to the exigencies of his existence. It is superstition that has made him a fool, it is religious tyranny that has enslaved his mind, perverted his faculties, and tarnished the glory of his intel-lectual energies. Christianity has taught him two awful and destructive lessons; first, that he is incapacitated for the per-formance of moral actions; and secondly in case he "should" perform them, they would add no merit or superior excel-lence to his character; that his best righteousness is like filthy rags which God would treat with marked abhorrence.

The repetition of such discouraging impressions must nec-essarily work an effect remarkably injurious to the virtuous activity of the human race. It is in conformity to this immoral instruction, that we see fanatic Christians every where boast-ing of their own inability, and doing violence to that inter-nal sentiment which would otherwise constantly impel them to the performance of acts of justice, benevolence, and uni-versal charity. In addition to the pointed declarations of the "holy scriptures" against the power and practice of morality, the inventors and promoters of the Christian religion have set up various kinds of doctrines, which diminish the motives to good actions, and lead the uninstructed mind to repose confi-dence in something foreign from its own exertions and merit, such as atonement, baptism, faith, sacramental suppers, obla-tions, and ablutions, together with many other idle ceremo-nies and wild vagaries of a distempered and fanatic brain.

The idea that Jesus the son of Mary died for the sins of the world, and that henceforth moral virtue can have no saving efficacy, is among the most destructive conceptions by which the moral world has been insulted and perverted. The supernatural grace of God, which Christians for so many ages have been in search of, has hitherto eluded the grasp of all rational and philosophic men; and to those who pretend to be acquainted with this celestial gift, it has been at times more trouble than profit; since innumerable doubts have been created concerning its reality and modes of operation in the human heart.

The cursory survey that has been taken of the immoral precepts and principles contained "in the Old and New Testament," clearly proves that these books are not of divine origin. The God of the Jews and Christians, according to their own description, is a changeable, passionate, angry, unjust, and revengeful being; infuriate in his wrath, capricious in his conduct, and destitute, in many respects, of those sublime and immutable properties which really belong to the Preserver of the universe. The characters spoken of in the scriptures, as the favorites of Heaven, such as Moses, Joshua, David, Solomon, Jesus, and Paul, are none of them good moral characters; it is not probable, therefore, that they were selected by the Creator as the organs of celestial communication. In the "Old Testament," national and individual justice is disregarded, and God is made the accomplice of crimes which human nature abhors. The maxims of the "New Testament" are a perversion of all correct principles in a code of moral virtue. The whole system is calculated to take man out of himself, to destroy his confidence in his own energies, to debase his faculties, vitiate his social affections, and brutalize the most useful qualities of human existence. The highest dignity of the human race consists in the practice of an exalted virtue, in the exercise of a fine sympathetic benevolence, in reciprocating our feelings and affections, in promoting the justice and order of society, in relieving the unfortunate and supporting the cause of truth, in diminishing evil and augmenting good; in short, in promoting universally the science, the virtue, and happiness of the world. There is, however, no possibility of faithfully performing these duties while under the shackles of Jewish and Christian superstition. The remedy consists in a return to nature, and in elevating our views and conceptions above those theological absurdities which have degraded man to a level with the beast, and taught him to respect his civil and ecclesiastical tyrants as beings of a higher order, or celestial messengers from a vindictive and revengeful God.

CHAPTER XII

Christian Martyrs, the Church, Opinions of Learned Divines

When all other arguments fail, we are called to contemplate the wonderful fortitude of those martyrs who have suffered and died in the cause of Christianity. Such religious heroism, it is said, could proceed only from a conscious certainty of the existence of those sublime and holy truths contained in the system that inspired such preternatural courage. The slightest knowledge of the history of the human passions would furnish a complete refutation of the argument in favor of revelation. Extravagant zeal and unbounded enthusiasm are frequently exhibited in many of the important concerns of human life; there are martyrs in the worst of causes, and if martyrdom could prove Christianity to be true, it would prove a hundred other things to be true which are in pointed opposition to that system. The Mahometan condemns the Christian, and the Christian condemns the Mahometan; their creeds are different, and in many respects contradictory; but they have both had martyrs without number; both systems have sacrificed millions upon the alter of theological fanaticism. Zeal among the Mahometans is not less infuriate nor less sincere, than among the Christians; and Mahometanism might as well be proved to be divine, from this kind of evidence, as the religion of Jesus. The historical fact is the same of all religions, especially of those which claim supernatural origin. Madmen and enthusiasts are to be found every where, and celestial enthusiasm is generally the most ranting and extravagant.

But when recurrence is made to the universal conduct of mankind in every age, and upon every important occasion, it is strange that an argument drawn from the conduct of Christian martyrs, should have been advanced in favor of the divine origin of this religion. The spirit of fanaticism, which made Europe, during several centuries, the slaughter-house of the world, will not, surely, be adduced in favor of the mild and celestial nature of the religion of Jesus; yet the crusades prove as much as individual martyrdom, and neither of these proves more than that human nature is susceptible of strong and rancorous passions, and that to the variety in the modification of these passions there is no end. A heated and delirious imagination always overturns the empire of reason, and subverts the throne of justice. The extent of real attachment which individuals may show towards any cause, in not conclusive evidence that such cause is right. It is evidence only, that such persons are deeply interested in it; but the interest which they take may be nourished by a thousand other causes, than a clear and comprehensive view of truth. The savage of America, has excelled in the patient fortitude of suffering beyond all that can be boasted by all the Christian martyrs of the world; yet this uncultivated man of the western world, holds in contempt the doctrines and promises of the Christian religion. It is directly in the face of all historical facts, to contend that the conduct of Christian martyrs substantiates, in any degree, the divinity of the Old or New Testament. From the banks of the Mississippi, to the island of Japan, there is not a spot of earth, but what has furnished martyrs in some cause or other; and if the idea contended for by believers, were true, it is certain that more than five hundred religious sectaries, all different in the tenets which they hold, could instantly prove the sacredness of their theological opinions, by reference to a spirit of fanatical martyrdom; which spirit, instead of bearing the least relation to truth, has served only to make man a miserable idiot, and deluge the world in blood.

The Church of Christ, in all ages, has come in for a share of influence and authority, to prove that the scriptures are true. "The Church has always believed in the Bible, and therefore the Bible is true. The Bible declares the Church to be right, and therefore the Church cannot be wrong; the Church proves the Bible, and the Bible proves the Church; thus the divinity of the one, and the infallibility of the other is rendered incontrovertible." If it were admitted that the authority or opinion of the Church could prove any thing, it would nevertheless be difficult to discover who are the Church. The sectarian divisions are so numerous, that it is impossible to determine which is the true Church. This would be a much more difficult task than to determine which is the erroneous Church. They continually dispute with each other concerning the truth of their doctrine, they anathematize one another, and are liberal in the charges of heresy; they are all heretics in the estimation of each other, and they have no standard to determine with certitude their theological differences. To bring the Church,

therefore, to prove the Christian religion, is to bring nothing at all, for nobody can tell who, or what the Church is. It
ought to be first settled which Church is to be relied on, or
rather which is to be considered as the true Church, and then
it would be time enough to decide whether even that one
had any just claim to settle for all mankind the problematical
points of truth and error. If, however, all the Churches in the
world, were agreed in their doctrines, this would not prove
them to be true; but amidst such ecclesiastical differences
of opinion, an honest enquirer of truth will find but little
consolation. These heterogeneous and contradictory ideas
upon supernatural theology necessarily destroy the validity and pretended divinity of all these systems. The Church
has carried every thing with a high hand, and attempted to
settle questions of truth by the force of authority; but force
has no relation to truth, and all authority of all the Churches
can never annihilate, in a single instance, the necessary and
essential connection between the truth of a proposition, and
the evidence by which it is supported. In former ages they
held many councils to decide upon ecclesiastical truths, and
at every successive council some alteration was made; truth
was never the same with them, and the final decisions were
regulated by the temperament, views, and interest of those
learned and pious clergymen, who composed those ecclesiastical associations. When the power of the councils was
not sufficient, the sword was resorted to, and this constituted
the "last reason" of the Church, as well as of kings. To histor-
ize the conduct of the Church, from the third century to the
commencement of the sixteenth, would fill many volumes,
and after all it would be nothing more that a dark history
of cruelty, force, persecution, burning of heretics, and shed-
ding, in the name of heaven, the blood of the human race.

If a corrupted Church and priesthood have believed in an error for a thousand years, this does not change the nature of that error, and cannot convert it into truth. "It is contended, that whoever calls in question the divinity of revealed religion, is flying in the face of the Church, and controverting its ancient and respectable opinions; that these opinions have stood the test of ages; that they have been believed by many pious and learned men, and cannot now be overturned by a new and infidel philosophy." To all this it may be answered, that a Church that has always been quarreling with itself concerning doctrines, is always to be suspected; it is absolutely necessary for the Church, first to settle its own disputes, before it calls others to account for unbelief. The bloody and ferocious conduct; the cruelties, differences, and persecutions of the Christian Church, in all ages, ought to destroy all its weight and authority. Truth has not been its object, for sincere inquiries after truth are disposed to mutual friendship and assistance; but this has never been the case with those religious despots, whose opinions have kept the world in an uproar for more than fifteen hundred years. It was at one a "famous" dispute among the clergy in Europe, "whether Jesus Christ was sitting, kneeling, or standing at the right hand of the Father in Heaven." This foolish and despicable altercation generated the most envenomed malice, and the most rancorous passions were let loose upon this occasion, to the destruction of order, peace, and human happiness. "But the Church is the repository of power; the Church knows every thing; the Church is always right, and woe be to that daring infidel who does not believe as the Church believes." It is high time for that reason of man to rise in all its energy, and sweep away such childish nonsense. "The opinions of the Church have stood the test of ages." But how, in what manner have they stood the test? as soon as the principles of science began to be investigated; as soon as philosophy had thrown off the shackles of authority, the opinions of the Church were called in question; revealed religion began to be doubted, and every supernatural system was subjected to a bold examination, which terminated against its truth and utility. In proportion as science advanced, infidelity has increased; in proportion as man has become acquainted with the nature of physical and moral principle, his respect for unnatural theology has constantly diminished. During fourteen hundred years of moral darkness, in which Europe was involved, it was impossible that the Christian religion should be brought to the test of a fair examination, and upright decision; the learning of those ages was almost exclusively confined to the clergy, and as they were universally attached, either from pure or interested motives, to the Christian religion, it was not possible that there should be any free inquiry upon the subject. It is very easy for a thing to stand the test where every body is in favor of it; this is exactly the case in regard to revealed religion; it stood the test very well when nobody had the sense or courage to oppose it. But when philosophy had opened her treasures, and developed some of the most sublime and important truths of nature; when reason had acquired strength, and taken the resolution to act for itself, "the test of ages" was shaken to its center. It is only within the last two centuries, that the great question concerning the truth of the Christian religion has been at all agitated; during this period, the contest has been always vastly unequal; the strength of civil and ecclesiastical despotism has been malignantly opposed to a peaceful and contemplative philosophy.

Notwithstanding all this, the progress has been great, error has been attacked on every side, new truths unfolded, and a door of consoling hope opened to the future generations of mankind; the opinions of pious and learned men ought never to be adduced to prove the celestial origin of the Christian religion. These same men, celebrated for piety and learning, have believed in the grossest absurdities, and the most childish errors. They have believed that the earth was the center of the planetary system, and that the sun constantly performed its revolution round it; whereas the reverse is the truth, the sun is the center of the planetary system, and round that resplendent luminary all the planets constantly revolve. They have believed in witchcraft, dreams, apparitions, and all that numerous train of ancient gentry, which have so much troubled the repose of credulous fools. Since then, it is certain, that they have submitted to the most childish and degrading credulity, their opinions cannot be cited in proof of any system whatever; they have been, however, honest, and in many instances, respectable men. Error is a misfortune and not a crime; but truth can never be substantiated by adducing, in support of it, the opinions of superstitious and deluded men.

CHAPTER XIII

Origin of Moral Evil, and the Means of Its Ultimate Extirpation from the Earth

The facts in the physical world are, many of them, difficult of solution; those of the moral world have perplexed still more the operations of the human understanding. The subtly, the abstruseness, the incognizable character of moral existence, place it beyond the power of clear intellectual perception, and the mind loses itself in those metaphysical combinations, whose successive variations are incalculable. But the difficulties which nature has thrown in the way of this inquiry are much less numerous than those presented by superstition. A design has been formed, and carried into effect, whose object it was to cover the moral world with a mantle of mystery, and exclude it wholly from the view of vulgar eyes, and common comprehension. It is only necessary to conceal the real nature and character of a thing, and then deformities and distortions may be made to pass for positive properties, or essential qualities inherent in any specific mode of existence. If the subtilty of thought, and the difficulty of moral discrimination, have in many cases presented to human investigation a barrier to farther

115

progress; the intentional malignant descriptions of super-stition have, in almost every age and country, terrified the mind of man, and prevented the development of substantial moral principle. Nature furnishes some difficulties, but supernatural theology exhibits many more.

In no one instance is this remark more substantially verified, than in the inquiries which man has made concerning the source or origin of moral evil. Reason and theology, philosophy and superstition, are at war upon this subject. The believers in the Christian religion, following the examples of their theological and fanatic predecessors, have searched the universe in quest of a satisfactory solution to that long alternated question – whence came moral evil? One religious sectary, willing to screen the divinity from any just accusation relative to so nefarious a concern, have descended into hell, and discovered there all the characters and distorted machinery necessary to the production of such an effect; but here metaphysical and fanatic invention indulged itself in all the extravagance of delusion. It was necessary first to create this "infernal" country, and then to create inhabitants suited to the nature of the climate, and the unfortunate condition in which they were to reside. The idea of a Devil was accordingly formed, and the reality of his existence rendered an indubitable truth by the reiterated assertions of superstition. Ignorance and fanaticism greedily swallowed the foolish "infernal" dose which had been administered.

There is a remarkable disposition in the human mind to remove the point of intellectual difficulty as far from the reality of the case as possible, and then it triumphantly imagines that a solution has been given. This is a fact particularly in theological inquiry, in which a few retrogressive efforts of the mind have been considered as an ample illustration of all the difficulties relative to the subject of Theism, and the existence of the physical universe. Similar to this idea is the doctrine concerning moral evil, and the disposition which theologians have exhibited to remove the burden from their own shoulders, and place it upon the devil's back. The whole "infernal" machinery with which we are presented by superstition, serves only to detach the mind from the true and real source of moral evil. While reflection is directed to another world, it is incompetent to a clear view of the facts existing in this, and the habit of such reveries produces a fanatic delirium subversive of all correctness of judgment. The existence of hell, and the beings that dwell therein, being only supported by what is called divine revelation, it follows, of course, that if this revelation is not true, a belief in any thing that is a mere result of that system cannot be substantially founded. Since then it is presumed, that in these chapters a competent refutation is given to the doctrine contained in the sacred books of the Jews and Christians, the idea of descending into hell, or having recourse to a devil, in search of moral evil, is futile and inconsistent.

Another part of the Christian world, willing to avoid difficulties which their antagonists had thrown in their way, abandoned the "infernal" abodes, and ascended into the celestial world, in quest of the origin of evil. They exhibited ingenious metaphysical reasoning upon the subject, declaring that God was the Creator of all things; that sin was something, and not nothing, and therefore he must be the Creator of sin or moral evil. This puzzled the advocates of the "hell scheme," and a clerical warfare was engendered concerning two theological opinions, neither of which had any kind of existence in the nature of things. After heaven and hell had been searched through and through to find something which did not belong to either of them, the terror-struck inquirer, as if fatigued with his atmospheric journey, seated himself once more upon the earth, and saw, or might have seen, in the very bosom of society, and the perverted character of man, a clear and satisfactory solution of that difficult question, which, for so long a time, had occupied his attention in distant regions. It is in this manner, that the plainest subject is rendered mysterious, when a superstitious religion is industriously employed in subverting the independent power of thought. It is neither in the upper nor lower regions; it is not in heaven nor in hell, that the origin of moral evil will be discovered; it is to be found only among those intelligent beings who exist upon the earth. "Man has created it, and man must destroy it."

But it is necessary to exhibit the proofs of this last assertion, and convince Christian theology of the innumerable errors, which for ages past have been imposed upon a credulous and deluded world. What is it, then, that constitutes a moral evil? It is the violation of a law of justice or utility, by any one of the human species, competent to distinguish between right and wrong. We have no other cognizable idea upon this subject. Facts and practice are presented continually to the view of the human mind; the decision of a correct mind is always according to the nature and character of the case. The character of a human being is made either good or bad by the actions he commits. If these actions are conformable to the principles of justice and universal benevolence, they are with great propriety denominated good; if they are unjust, cruel, and destructive to sensitive and intellectual life, they are denominated bad. There are certain fundamental laws, suitable for the government of rational being, and it is a departure from these laws that vitiates the human character. It is proved in another part of this work, that virtue and vice are personal qualities, and that they result from personal adherence to, or personal infraction of moral law.

It is only necessary in this place to call the attention once more to the nature of human actions, and to the characteristic difference between them, in order to establish the position principally assumed in this inquiry; for it ought to be recollected, that even if it "could" be proved, which by the way it cannot, that even a deity or a devil had violated moral law, this would not effect the decision upon the subject in regard to man; because that evil could not be transferred from a different kind of being in the other world, to those who exist upon earth. As the moral properties of all intelligent agents are personal; are essentially their own and not another's; as there can be no justifiable transfer between man and man, so it follows that there can be none between man and devil. Every intellectual being must depend upon himself; must rest upon his own energies and be responsible for himself. Man must, therefore, relinquish that position, which has been assumed by Christian theology, relative to the transferable nature of moral qualities. Christianity presents us with two grand leading characters, to whom we are always referred in our inquiries upon the subject of moral evil. Adam and Jesus are these persons, and in them is said to have been concentrated the sin and righteousness of the human race. The new Testament declares that, "as in Adam all die, even so in Christ shall all be made alive." This is a sweeping clause, in regard to the moral existence of man, and flies in the face of universal experience. Facts are at war with this scriptural declaration, and it is impossible to reduce the sentiment to practice, without producing in common life the grossest violations of justice. Admitting for a moment the existence of such a man as Adam, which by the way is extremely problematical, it will not follow, that there was in him either a moral or physical death of the human race. Physically it is impossible, and morally it is unjust. If Christian theology has made a recurrence to Adam, to aid the solution of difficulties, relative to the origin of moral evil; if it has by this idea perverted the eternal principles of discriminative justice, it has also been equally unfortunate in calling in the righteous Jesus to its assistance, in expectation of ultimately destroying the immorality of the world. The scriptures invite us to behold the Lamb of God, that taketh away the sins of the world. The Lamb is Jesus, the only begotten of the Father; he is reputed to be divine and uncontaminated with any kind of moral turpitude. His is made the victim of Jehovah's wrath, and falls a sacrifice to the vindictive fury of his benevolent father, and all this for the purpose of removing crimes for which apostate man should have been scourged and afflicted. Means more unsuitable or incompetent to the production of such an effect, could never have been invented by the delirious brain of fanaticism itself; but the absurd and incompetent methods which Christian theology has invented for the destruction of moral evil, are not so much the objects of the present investigation, as the means which reason has in view to effectuate the moral renovation of the species. It is a common complaint among theological doctors, that the "world is growing worse and worse."[1]

Passing by any strictures upon the ill compliment which theologists pay to themselves by indulging such a sentiment,

---

1 See chapter on Death, or the disorganization of intelligent beings.

the truth of the opinion itself will become a more important matter of discussion. The organic construction, the powers and the properties of human existence, the aggregate amount of virtue and vice in the present generation, these are objects subjected to the inspection of the human mind; but the conduct and character of man, in former ages, is to be drawn from history. Histories, however, are not always faithful to the realities of the case, and description is sometimes excessive and sometimes deficient. But judging from what we know, and including in the ground of decision, similarity of organic structure, cogent proofs will be exhibited against the admission of an opinion hostile to the ultimate perfectibility of intelligent life. The expansion of mind, the development of principles, and the cultivation of the arts, in a degree far superior to all the specimens of high antiquity, evince an incontrovertible amelioration in the present race. The accommodations favorable to the comfort and happiness of life, with which man has surrounded himself, demonstrate that there exists in the constitution of his nature a strong and indestructible impulse to progressive improvement; to the diminution of evil, and the augmentation of good. The fine moral qualities of the heart, which adorn cultivated life, give to it a splendid brilliancy, and triumphant exaltation above the coarse, instinctive brutality of former ages. If personal malignity and national warfare continue, the first is diminished in the acrimony of its character, and the second has regulated its movements, in some measure, upon the principles of a reciprocal humanity, and a greater respect for the dignity of human existence. These are facts with which we are every moment presented in the history of modern times; those who controvert these assertions must have forgotten, or never knew, the names of Alexander, of Nero, and Caligula; of the numerous ecclesiastical despots and persecutors with which the history of the Christian Church presents us, anterior to the commencement of the sixteenth century; nay farther, they must have neglected the reading of the "Holy Scripture," and have lost sight of the character of Moses, that eminent murderer of antiquity. The Mahometan arguments in favor of belief must also have escaped their notice; in short, the advocates of pre-eminent virtue in former ages have shut their eyes against the history of kings and priests; against the knowledge of those dreadful effects, which the compound despotism of the church and state has produced upon the human race.

If the modern "Suwarrow" be brought as an example of refutation of these remarks, it is admitted in its full force, and this eminent murderer of modern times is consigned, by the sentiment of humanity, to the grave of eternal infamy. But the cases of such savage barbarity are growing less numerous in proportion as the knowledge of principle advances, and the correspondent moral practice flowing from such knowledge. Reason, or the intellectual powers of man, must eventually become both the deposit and the guardian of the rights and happiness of human existence. Reason has already acquired such strength, and so far unfolded its powers, that it has already sealed the future destiny of the human race. It is the peculiar office of reason to look to the utter demolition of the ancient regimen of church and state. These twin sisters of iniquity are the moral giants, which have stalked with huge devastation over the face of the whole globe. Political despotism and supernatural religion have done more to render the human race vicious and depraved, than all other causes conjointly combined. If the passions of man and the impulses of his nature have frequently produced a moral eccentricity in his conduct, it is certain that a corrupt government and a corrupt religion have rendered him habitually wicked; have perverted all the conceptions of the mind upon moral and political subjects, and brutalized his intellectual existence.

The most important step which can be taken for the extermination of vice and misery, is to destroy the artificial causes by which such evils are perpetrated. If other causes should be found to exist in the constitution of nature, they will be progressively removed by the light and power of science, and a more comprehensive view of the true interest of the human species. But efforts tending to make the individuals of a nation virtuous and happy, will never succeed extensively till the civil and religious tyranny under which they groan shall be completely annihilated. This will lead to the application of force in the political revolutions of the world; an expedient, however, the rectitude of which some benevolent philosophers have called in question. An ample discussion of this point, however, is reserved to occupy a place in a political work, which the author is preparing for the press, and which will be presented to the view of the public as soon as it is completed.

It is sufficient at this time to remark, that despotism gives no encouragement to any kind of improvement, and the hope of human amelioration from this quarter will ever prove to be fallacious. Reason, righteousness and immortal reason, with the argument of the printing types in one hand, and the keen argument of the sword in the other, must attack the thrones and the hierarchies of the world, and level them with the dust of the earth; then the emancipated slave must be raised by the power of science into the character of an enlightened citizen; thus possessing a knowledge of his rights, a knowledge of his duties will consequently follow, and he will discover the intimate and essential union between the highest interests of existence, and the practice of an exalted virtue. If civil and ecclesiastical despotism were destroyed, knowledge would become universal, and its progress inconceivably accelerated. It would be impossible, in such a case, that moral virtue should fail of a correspondent acceleration, and the ultimate extirpation of vice would become an inevitable consequence. Ages must elapse before the accomplishment of an object so important to the elevated concerns of intelligent life; but the causes are already in operation, and nothing can arrest or destroy the benignant effects which they are calculated to produce. The power of reason, the knowledge of printing, the overthrow of political and ecclesiastical despotism, the universal diffusion of the light of science, and the universal enjoyment of republican liberty; these will become the harbingers and procuring causes of real virtue in every individual, and universal happiness will become the lot of man.

CHAPTER XIV

Infidel Philosophy

The discovery of the art of printing was a deadly blow to religious fanaticism, and to every species of error. The clergy rejoiced in this discovery, but their rejoicing was an untimely delusion of the heart; they were blind to the consequences of this fortunate and consoling discovery. The consideration of exhibiting, in a new form, the sublime and holy truths of the Christian religion, was to them a matter of the most elevated satisfaction, and they anticipated a result directly the reverse of what has taken place. It was believed, that a religion sent from heaven to benefit only a small part of the human race, would have been always confined within the power and discretion of a privileged and ecclesiastical order. To this sacred hand learning had been hitherto been confined, and it was perceived that the art of printing was calculated to break the charm, and diffuse among the nations of the earth a moral light, consoling to the heart of ignorant and unfortunate man. Such, however, was the result, and the human mind received and experienced a new and powerful motive to energize its powers and provide for its happiness. Many important causes combined at one and the same time to excite fresh vigor, and increase the activity of intellectual strength. The ecclesiastical dissensions in Europe; the discovery of the new world; the discovery of the art of printing; the philosophical investigations of French, English, and German philanthropists; all these, and many other powerful circumstances, were concentrated, and produced a new era in the intellectual history of man.

Newton, profiting by the errors of those great philosophers, Descartes and Bacon; Newton, whose original genius and comprehensive mind have immortalized his name and character, developed with clearness the physical principles and order of the planetary system, and struck with everlasting death and eternal silence the theological pretension of all former ages. The ignorance and stupidity of Moses, Joshua,, and Jesus, were exposed, and their opinions were sacrificed upon the alter of philosophical truth and mathematical demonstration. Newton's mind was honest and discerning, but partially obscured by the moral darkness of the age in which he lived, and the theological impressions of early life. He was reputed to be a Christian upon a graduated scale; but the habit of mathematical precision had led him to a rejection of the doctrine of the trinity, and some other prominent absurdities in the theology of Christians. His discoveries, however, in the physical world, were vastly important to the cause of human science, and have been productive of a more accurate mode of reasoning, than any that had been adopted in former ages. The demonstrations of Newton were compared to the theological reveries of Moses and Joshua. The consequences of which was, that the scientific philosopher rejected the imaginary conceptions of fanaticism, and bestowed on solid argument a due portion of respect and attachment.

It was not the discovery of physical truths alone that bore relation to the renovation of the human species; it was reserved for Locke, and other powerful minds, to unfold the internal structure of the intellectual world; explain the operations of the human understanding; explore the sources of thought, and unite sensation and intellect in the same subject, and in a manner cognizable by the human faculties. Locke has, perhaps, done more than Newton, to subvert the credit of "divine Revelation;" but neither of them discovered the extent of the doctrines upon the moral interests of man. Sensation being established as the source and cause of all human ideas, a system of true and material philosophy necessarily followed. Organization was, of course, considered essential to the production of intellect, and disorganization bearing very hard against a conscious reminiscence of identified existence, speculations upon the doctrines concerning futurity became frequent, and the ultimate decision rested upon the discoveries which had been made in human sensation. In addition to these leading features of a sound philosophy destined to emancipate the world from a religious bondage, other collateral and subsequent aids were experienced, and had a powerful effect in ameliorating the moral condition of society. Mirabaud, Rousseau, Voltaire, Hume, and Bolingbroke, together with twenty other philosophers of France and England, combined their strength in the philanthropic cause of human improvement; they destroyed error by wholesale, and swept away the rubbish of ancient superstition, by the irresistible force of a keen and active intelligence. Those moral luminaries were followed by those of more modern times, and the present age is preeminently distinguished by a numerous and respectable band of philanthropic philosophers, whose labors are calculated to destroy error, and elevate truth upon the ruins of every thing injurious to the peace and dignity of human society.

The writings of Paine bear the most striking relation to the immediate improvement and moral felicity of the intelligent world. He writes upon principle, and he always understands the principle on which he writes; he reasons with logic, and convinces with argumentation; he strangles error by his first grasp, and develops truth with much simplicity, but with irresistible force. He is one of the first and best of writers, and probably the most useful man that ever existed upon the face of the earth. His moral and political writings are equally excellent, and the beneficial influence of the principles for which he has contended, will be felt through all succeeding ages.

Volney and Condorcet, Godwin and Barlow, are justly entitled to the universal gratitude and applause of the human race. They have attacked error in its strongest holds; they have pursued it with a powerful and discriminating intellect. It has already lost half of its force; and the philosophy that is denominated infidel, will, ere long, chase it out of existence. It is this philosophy that has developed the laws of the physical world, and exhibited the principles on which its systematic order depends; it is this philosophy that has unfolded the moral energies of human nature, which has become an object of calumny in the estimation of a cruel and persecuting superstition.

All the opprobrious epithets in the English language have been bestowed upon that mild and peaceful philosophy, whose object is the discovery of truth, and whose first wish is to emancipate the world from the double despotism of church and state. This philosophy has already destroyed innumerable errors; it has disclosed all the fundamental principles which have been employed in the construction of machines, mathematical instruments, and the arrangement of those moral and political systems which have softened the savage and ferocious heart of man, and raised the ignorant slave from the dust, into the elevated character of an enlightened citizen. Its only weapons are thought, contemplation, argument, demonstration, experiment, and probable conjecture; whilst, on the other hand, the only weapons of despotism are "cold steel," or "leaden balls." This despotism, however, whether it be political or ecclesiastical, is malignantly employed in opposing and calumniating that philosophy, which has sought with an ardent benevolence for the scientific improvement of man, and the tranquillity of nations. The philosophy of Europe armed itself with a spirit of truth and the sword of justice; it humanely marched forth to conquer the errors and vices of nations, and restore to man his lost dignity, which had long ago been sacrificed upon the alter of theological fanaticism. This effort, propelled by wisdom and humanity, was denounced by the thundering voice of the church, and the resentful malice of monarchical tyranny.

The "Illuminati" in Europe have been represented as a vicious combination of persons, whose object was the destruction of all the governments and religions of the world. If the enemies of philosophy, in that part of the globe, mean by governments the corrupt monarchies of the earth, and by religion, popular superstition, founded upon the idea of a supposed mysterious intercourse between beings of the earth and celestial powers, then they are right in this respect; for these are the governments and religions against which reason and philosophy ought to direct their energies; but if by government they mean a system of genuine republicanism, founded upon the equal rights of man, and by religion the idea of simple Theism, and the immortality of moral virtue, then their assertions are false, and their productions a calumny against reason and the rights of human nature. The plain truth of the case is, that those who oppose philosophy, and bestow upon it harsh and malignant epithets, are interested in keeping up a privileged system of plunder and robbery, which make nine-tenths of the human race absolute slaves, to support the other tenth in indolence, extravagance, pride and luxury. The purest systems of morals that could possibly be exhibited, and the demonstrable axioms of the soundest philosophy, would become objects of unbounded reproach, and their abettors marked as objects of the bitterest censure, if the ancient regimen of church and state were to be in any shape whatever injured by such development. The physical force of nations would be drawn forth to suppress the independent power of thought, destroy damnable heresy, and arrest, in the name of heaven, those infidel philosophers, whose efforts had been directed to the emancipation and moral felicity of these malicious and tyrannical persecutors. The cry of vengeance and merciless punishment against the benevolent philosophers of all countries of the present day has not deterred them from the faithful discharge of their duty, and the most unremitting attention to the best interest of individual and national happiness. The strong arm of despotism can never reach the subtle activity of thought, or subvert the dignified empire of reason. It is now the object of despotism to stop the progress of intellect, or prevent the universal diffusion of useful knowledge. The substantial happiness of the human species depends upon the activity of reason, and the liberty of the press; they have gained too much strength to be crushed by all the civil and religious tyranny of the world.

CHAPTER XV

Inquiry, Are the Evils Incident to Human Life the Result of the Operation of the Laws of Nature; or Are They Special Judgments from God?

M an will never cease to be erroneous in his reasonings, while he departs from the simple and uniform ground of nature; the only solid basis of all conclusive argumentation, the only true source of all important science. It is in the physical constitution of existence in its real relations, in its energies, in its effects, that he must seek for principles by which to construct a useful and well cemented fabric; by which to arrange and methodize thought, and apply it to the diversified purposes of human life. The imperfection of his faculties does not enable him to seize upon all these objects in such a manner to preclude the possibility, and even probability of many errors; but these errors are to be destroyed only by a constant recurrence to the fundamental "data," from which correct conclusions must ever be deduced.

Man has lost himself in the wanderings of a fantastic imagination, in the fleeting dreams of fanaticism, and the malignant fury of a blind superstition; he has sought for truth where it is not to be found, his mind has diverged from the line of reality, and he has become the victim of innumerable prejudices. The most common phenomena have been ascribed to causes which had no existence, and effects have been attributed to those chimerical combinations which were to be found only in the distorted brain of an enthusiastic religious zealot. The simplicity, the uniformity, the grandeur of the physical universe, have been abandoned, while the fictions and non- entities of delirious mortals have been substituted as the ground of evidence, and the principle of correct conclusion. It was not in the organization of the material world, that man sought for truth, but in the deceptive schemes of religion, which interested zeal imposed upon him.

The sensation, the intellect, the capacities of man, taught him that he was subject to a variety of evils; but instead of searching for the cause of these evils, where only they were to be found, he suffered the operations of intellect to be subjugated by the pride and arrogance of superstition, and he no longer discerned the true connection between the miseries which he felt, and the active and natural causes which produced them; he no longer beheld his true condition in nature, but weakly imagined that he had become the object of malevolent intention in some superior being, who took delight in his torture, and willfully subjected him to the diversified misfortunes with which he was assailed. In this unfortunate predicament, with too much weakness to abandon his errors, and too much prejudice to discover the truth, he wandered over the face of

Nature, the devoted victim of that ignorance and

superstition which for so long a time had destroyed the tranquility of his heart, and suppressed the operation of his mind; he inquired with anxious solicitude into the causes of his sufferings; he sought in a vindictive theology for a solution of the difficulty, but his inquiry ended in an accumulation of sorrow, and a repetition of the misfortunes from which in vain he had endeavored to escape. By dint of investigation, by constancy of intellectual inquiry, he at length was led to discover, that the evils which he suffered were to be accounted for by a single comparison and application of the law of power in surrounding objects, and the law of sensation, by which his life was every moment modified; the development and explanation of this solid truth will constitute the true ground of the present inquiry.

While physical existence continues what it now is, while its powers, its modes of operation, its essential energies remain the same, it will be impossible to modify a sensible being so as to prevent his being necessarily subjected to a diversity of unpleasant and painful sensations. Power and activity are essential to the existence of matter, and capacity of sensation to every specific modification of life; an undue proportion of this power, applied to any sensitive agent, will necessarily damage, in some partial degree, the natural organization of which he is possessed; it is the nature of life to feel, to be sensible, to be capable of perception; it is the nature of physical objects to make impressions, and if the impressions from surrounding objects are not properly apportioned to the capacity of sensation, the natural result will be pain, distress, or complete misery, according to the nature and quantity of that power which in any case may be applied; such consequences must inevitably follow, while the law of power in physical objects, and the law of sensation in modified life, maintain the same relation which they now bear to each other. It will, therefore, be for ever impossible wholly to prevent pain, unless you destroy the law of power in material nature, or the law of sensation in animal life. The relation and connection now subsisting between them, necessarily includes the possibility, and even the absolute certainty of the existence of pain, or some portion of real misery. It will be perceived, in this method of reasoning, that every idea of suspension or violation of the laws of nature is excluded, and that identity of power and quality in specific portions of nature is presumed to be perpetuated with undeviating uniformity.

To show the correctness of this opinion, it is only necessary to have recourse to a few familiar examples in the ordinary concerns of human life; for instance, if a man were to thrust his hand into the fire, or if by any other means fire should come in contact with any part of a sensitive being, the feeling experienced must necessarily be painful, because the law of power or activity in fire, and the law of sensation in modified life, necessarily includes the impossibility of preventing such consequence. Again, if any one were situated so that a heavy body falling from above should come directly upon him, it would be impossible to prevent disorganization or death, unless the law of gravitation were suspended, or his own peculiar structure of body instantaneously changed. In short, the whole application of the power of physical existence to the condition of sensitive creatures will ever prove, that such necessary consequences must be experienced.

Look through the whole order of nature, and this solemn truth is clearly perceived, that every being possessed of feeling must eternally be exposed to a vast variety of complicated evils, painful sensation, and diversified misfortune, resulting from the constitution of the universe, and the laws by which it is governed. The same reasoning will apply to all the higher operations of nature, and those astonishing phenomena that surprise and terrify the mind of man! Earthquakes, volcanoes, lightning, inundations, are all the result of the operation of physical laws, and it is impossible to prevent the misery which they occasion, without a suspension or violation of the laws by which they were produced.

A similar mode of reasoning will partially apply in regard to those evils that attack associated bodies of men, where superabundance of population, with a variety of other causes, has laid the foundation of inevitable disease, such as plagues, malignant fevers, and many others to which large and populous cities are subjected. But this part of the subject requires particular examination, since it is here that superstition has raised a rampart impregnable to the attacks of reason. The pride, the fanaticism, and the intemperate zeal of man will never cease to mislead his judgment; cause the energies of intellect to diverge from the line of truth, and to subject him to the baneful influence of opinions, erroneous and destructive in their consequences. Man is ignorant, and this ignorance produces in him an attachment to the marvelous; he is both delighted and terrified with strange and unnatural appearances, with events out of the common order of things, with those phenomena which approach or seem to approach the idea of a miraculous occurrence; he seems to take a pride also in attributing these events to the special interventions of Divine Providence, to the supernatural operations of a vindictive God; to the cruel and arbitrary arrangements of an omnipotent tyrant, to the malice and premeditated revenge of that ferocious being, who exists only in his own distorted imagination, and the admission of whose existence would be the sure presage of the annihilation of the vast fabric of nature. The fanaticism and intemperate zeal of all supernatural religion has ever desired to represent the God of nature as partial in his operations, revengeful in his intentions, and inconsiderately destructive in all those arrangements of which he is supposed to be the author and contriver. All the various religious parties and sectaries that have ever existed on earth, have pretended that God was enlisted in their service, and consequently, that he had proclaimed war, and the most implacable resentment against every other man or set of men who had not embraced the true and orthodox faith.

This terrible representation of the divinity, as destitute of truth as it was pernicious in its consequences, was, at length, diversified and decompounded, and afterwards recombined for purposes of systematic terror; the partial distribution of favors, and the dreadful torture of the human race under the name of divine vengeance. The professors of different religious opinions having armed their God in their own cause, became the merciless distributors of those dreadful punishments and calamities which they expected would result from the character of that barbarous divinity, which their imaginations had described. The malice of the individual, the savage cruelty of man, was transferred to this imaginary God, and he appeared in turn the object of terror to every living mortal. Man thus wishing to gratify his resentment against his neighbor, of an opposite religious opinion, has never failed to engage his God in is own quarrels; and if in the course of events, if any misfortune befell his enemy, the doctrine of special providence was then verified in his mind, and he triumphantly asserted that the Almighty had made bare the arm of his justice, and brought ruin and destruction upon the objects of his wrath. This doctrine, so humiliating to the character of man, and so disgraceful to the intelligent preserver of nature, has been fundamental in every religious system of supernatural origin. It took its rise in the weakness and malevolence of human nature, and its destructive consequences will have no end, till reason shall enlighten and renovate the world.

To expose the absurdity of this doctrine, it is only necessary to have recourse to the plainest facts, and the incontestable evidence resulting from a view of those events which are every where presented to the contemplation of man. If in any of those cases which include the admission of a special providence, recurrence were made to the most obvious and striking truths, the error must inevitably be corrected. If plagues, malignant fevers, or national calamities of any kind be considered as the scourges of divine vengeance for the punishment of sin, why do they fall indiscriminately upon the virtuous and the vicious, upon the young and the old, upon the weak and the strong, in fact, upon every class of intelligent beings, whatever may be their character, their circumstances, and condition in life? Why does not divine justice apportion these punishments to the actual degree of criminality in each individual that is made the object of is displeasure? Why does he not pour out his beneficence upon the chosen children of his love, and mark with tokens of displeasure those only who are his real enemies, those only who are disobedient and incorrigibly wicked? But no! this is not the manner of his operation; this arrangement of distributive justice is no where to be discovered. The child of God, and the child of the devil, are often involved in the same calamity; frequently subjected to the same disease, and eventually fall a sacrifice to the same complaint. This proves that the event has been produced by the uniform operations of the laws of nature, and not by any special judgment from God; this proves incontestably, a want of moral discrimination, and overturns every argument which Superstition has arranged for the accomplishment of her wicked intentions.

Whoever will deign to look at facts, will be necessitated to yield to the truth of these operations; they stand verified by observation, by the universal experience of all mankind. There is not, perhaps, a single case in which man reasons so much in the face of facts, as in the admission of a special providence in the government of the world. These reflections, though they may at first appear to operate against the cause of virtue, will, when attentively examined, be found to produce an opposite effect, and present to the human mind the strongest induce-ments to the practice of genuine morality; for no one can with justice pretend that the discovery and the disclosure of truth can injure the moral improvement of the species; and although the world is governed by general laws, and consequently every description of character is necessarily involved in the result of their operation, yet it is also certain, that the design and the practice of virtue are the surest grounds on which to rest the expectation of moral felicity. It is true, indeed, that no degree of virtue can effectually secure man against the effects of physical evil; because whatever may be the excellence of his character, this excellence will not prevent the uniformity of operation in the material world, nor change the immutable laws by which it is governed, nor can it destroy that universal relation which every where exists between sensation and the law of power in external objects. In vain shall we search for a solution of dif-ficulties in the mutable decrees of a capricious divinity: it will ever be necessary to have a recourse to the fundamental laws by which the material universe is regulated; it will ever be necessary to abide faithfully by the universal principles of nature in all our decisions on this important subject.

No system can more effectually disgrace the moral character of God, than that which includes the idea of partial arrangement in the government of the world; and no system is more incontestably proved by facts, than that which admits universality of operation in the whole of physical existence. The evils of which man complains, and which he unphilosophically denominates the judgments of God, are consequences resulting from the establishment of immutable laws; and the want of moral discrimination relative to the suffering objects, verifies this principle incontrovertibly.

It is further to be considered what terrible consequences would flow from the doctrine of special judgments. This doctrine practically forbids benevolent intention, and would frequently incriminate the efforts of humanity in relieving distress, and mitigating the circumstances of the unfortunate. If it be the will of the Divinity to pour out his wrath upon a whole city, and to destroy its inhabitants by malignant fevers, who shall dare to oppose his determination? Who shall presume to exercise the healing art, when Heaven decrees sickness and death? Who shall be found hardy enough to enter the lists with the Creator, and attempt to avert his judgment? In short, if this doctrine were admitted and reduced to practice, it would destroy, in some of the most essential cases, all the friendly and social virtues of man, and brutalize the human race. But, fortunate for man, if in theory he hold this doctrine sacred, his practical conduct humanely varies from the theory. The smallest recurrence to facts in the single instance of malignant fevers, would clearly substantiate this assertion. Superstition may darken the mind and derange its theoretic speculation, but the benevolence of the heart rises superior to these doleful illusions, and delights in the performance of duty.

In vain then do you speak of special judgments to that man whose family is attacked with malignant disease: he practically denies the truth of the doctrine, and humanely proceeds, as he ought, to administer the proper and necessary relief; even those who pretend to believe in this manifestation of divine vengeance, are often the first to oppose the will of Heaven, and restore health to a distracted family. Whence this difference between doctrine and action, between theory and practice? Will man never learn to be consistent, will he never forsake his errors and return to nature? It is on this grand system alone that he can find consolation; it is here only that the ardent desires of his heart can be satisfied, and confidence restored to his soul. Every deviation from nature is the establishment of a cause which must sooner or later work ruin to his sensations, or essentially disturb the tranquility of his mind; he will find no happiness in error, and the most dreadful of all his errors is to be found in the terrible descriptions of the Divinity that he worships; he falsely attributes to this Divinity the diversified evils which he himself has produced, and while he remains under the impression of such an opinion, he will be for ever ignorant of the true sources of those miseries to which he is continually exposed.

"How long will man importune the heavens with unjust complaints? How long with vain clamors will he accuse fate as the author of his calamities? Will he then never open his eyes to the light, and his heart to the insinuations of truth and reason? This truth every where presents itself in radiant brightness, and he does not see it! the voice of reason strikes his ear; and he does not hear it! Unjust man! If you can for a moment suspend the delusions which fascinates your senses; if your heart be capable of comprehending the language of argumentation, interrogate nature."

"In what consists the maledictions of heaven against these countries? Where is the divine curse that perpetuates this scene of desolation? Monuments of past ages! say, have the heavens changed their laws; and the earth its course? Has the sun extinguished his fires in the regions of space? Do the seas no longer send forth clouds? Are the rain and the dew fixed in the air? Do the mountains retain their springs? Are the streams dried up? And do the plants no more bear fruit and seed? Answer, race of falsehood and iniquity! Has God troubled the primitive and invariable order, which he himself assigned to nature? Has heaven denied to the earth, and the earth to its inhabitants, the blessings that were formerly dispensed! If the creation has remained the same, if its sources and its instruments are exactly what they once were, wherefore should not the present race have every thing within their reach that their ancestors enjoyed? Falsely do you accuse fate and the divinity; injuriously refer to God the cause of your evils."

"Tell me, perverse and hypocritical race, if these places are desolate, if powerful cities are reduced to solitude, is it he that has occasioned the ruin? Is it his hand that has thrown down these walls, sapped these temples, mutilated these pillars? Or is it the hand of man? Is it the arm of God that has introduced the sword into the city, and set fire to the country, murdered the people, burned the harvests, rooted up the trees, and ravaged the pastures? Or is it the arm of man? And when, after this devastation, famine has started up, is it the vengeance of God that has sent it, or the mad fury of mortals? When, during the famine, the people are fed with unwholesome provisions, and pestilence ensues, is it inflicted by the anger of heaven, or brought about by human imprudence? When war, famine, and pestilence united, have swept away the inhabitants, and the land has become a desert, is it God who has depopulated it? Is it his rapacity that plunders the laborer, ravages the productive fields, and lays waste the country; or the rapacity of those who govern? It is his pride that creates murderous wars, or the pride of kings and their ministers? Is it the venality of his decisions that overthrows the fortune of families, or the venality of the organs of the law? Are they his passions that; under a thousand forms, torment individuals and nations, or the passions of human beings? And if in the anguish of their misfortunes they perceive not the remedies, is it the ignorance of God that is in fault, or their own ignorance? Cease, then, to accuse the decrees of fate, or the judgments of heaven! If God is good, will he be the author of your punishment? No, no; the caprice of which man complains, is not the caprice of destiny; the darkness that misleads his reason, is not the darkness of God; the source of his calamities is not in the distant heavens, but near to him upon the earth; it is not concealed in the bosom of the divinity; it resides in himself, man bears it in his heart."

"You murmur and say, Why have an unbelieving people enjoyed the blessings of Heaven and of earth? Why is a holy and chosen race less fortunate than impious generations? Deluded man! where is the contradiction at which you take offense? Where is the inconsistency in which you suppose the justice of God to be involved? Take the balance of blessings and calamities, of causes and effects, and tell me, when those infidels observed the laws of the earth and the heavens, when they regulated their intelligent labors by the order of the seasons, and the course of the stars, ought God to have troubled the equilibrium of the world to defeat their prudence? When they cultivated with care and toil the face of the country around you, ought he to have turned aside the rain to have withheld the fertilizing dews, and caused thorns to spring up?"

"When to render this parched and barren soil productive, their industry constructed aqueducts, dug canals, and brought the distant waters across the deserts; ought he to have blighted the harvests which art had created; to have desolated a country that had been peopled in peace; to have demolished the towns which labor had caused to flourish; in fine, to have deranged and confounded the order established by the wisdom of man? And what is this 'infidelity', which founded empires by prudence, defended them by courage, and strengthened them by justice; which raised magnificent cities, formed vast ports, drained pestilential marshes, covered the seas with ships, the earth with inhabitants, and, like the creative spirit, diffused life and motion through the world? If such is impiety, what is true belief?"(1) [1. See Volney's "Ruins," page 23, et seq.]

The correct and unprejudiced observer of nature, the genuine moralist, will necessarily accede to the truth of the above remarks, and in all his reasonings he will analyze facts, and attribute events to the real causes which have produced them; he will be under the necessity of rejecting those senseless opinions which have never failed to involve human inquiries in the doleful predicament of endless contradictions and absurdity. There can be no errors more pernicious than those which destroy the uniformity of operation in the physical world, and despoil the Creator of the honor of governing the universe by immutable laws. So long as the belief of special judgments shall obtain, man will for ever tremble before a capricious tyrant, who deserves neither gratitude nor admiration; but if the evils of life be attributed to their true sources, he will learn to provide against them, and to found his happiness upon a comprehensive view and knowledge of those principles by which the conservation of all existence is rendered sure and certain to every intelligent being. Prophecies, miracles, special judgments, and divine vengeance, are phrases without meaning, and phantoms without existence, calculated only to disgrace the character of God, and derange the intellectual faculties of man. Philosophy teaches us to seek in nature, and the knowledge of her laws, for the cause of every event, and when this knowledge shall become universal, man will relinquish with elevated satisfaction his attachment to those supernatural schemes of a vindictive theology, which have served only to destroy the harmony of nature, and demoralize the intelligent world. O, man! return in thy inquiries to the basis of physical existence, develope its principles, cultivate science, love truth, practice justice, and thy life shall be rendered happy.

CHAPTER XVI

Christian Devil

In the examination of the Christian religion, it would be improper to pass over, in silence, a character of so much power and importance as that of the devil. If accounts are true, he has acted a very conspicuous part upon the theater of theological delusion. He was the leader of a refractory band of insurgents in the celestial world; a vast and tremendous conflict ensued, in which it became necessary for Jehovah to draw forth all his forces to quell the rioters. It was with difficulty that this grand object was accomplished by the united exertions of the angelic hosts, under the guidance of the most distinguished officers of the upper regions.

Milton has described in a terrific manner these heated and resentful combats, and given to the most enthusiastic fictions the character and effect of real existence. His poetic fancy, the extent of his imagination, and brilliancy of conception, have been, and will long continue to be, admired; but his Paradise Lost, in the estimation of sound philosophy, and considered in its relation to philosophical truth, is an object of censure and contempt. He has done more to immortalize the marvelous character of a fictitious being, than even the Bible itself. He has given to "airy phantoms, a local habitation, and a name." The Christian devil is seen performing very marvelous feats in several different places in the Bible. He has vast powers of modifying his form and appearance, and can exhibit himself in an infinite variety of shapes. He assumes the form of a serpent, and very cunningly introduces himself to the original mother of the human race. It is in this fanciful scene so dexterously played off in the garden of Eden, that commenced the innumerable troubles, and destructive evils, that have since overwhelmed the life of man, and rendered miserable the fair creation of God. In almost all the cases where the Devil has brought his powers into vigorous action, he has succeeded, in despite and defiance even of Omnipotence itself. God made the world for his own glory, for the purposes of virtue and felicity, but the Devil overturned the scheme, before it had come fairly into operation; and thus, in the very commencement of the business, defeated the wisdom, and disordered the creation of the "Most High." It is very extraordinary that a being of perfect wisdom and goodness, whose object must have been to extend the empire of happy and intelligent life, should have made such bad calculation, and so soon have been deranged in the correctness and benevolence of his designs.

It is remarkable, that in the sentences of condemnation which were passed upon the several offenders, there is a difficulty and singularity in that which relates to the the serpent. "And the Lord God said unto the serpent, because thou hast done this, thou art cursed above all cattle, and above every beast of the field; upon thy belly shalt thou go, and dust shalt thy eat all the days of thy life." It is a question of magnitude, which ought to engage the attention of theological doctors to inform us, in what manner the serpent performed locomotion, previous to his transgression, for which he received the condemnatory sentence of going upon his belly. Did he walk about erect like a man? if so, he must have cut a curious figure, travelling about upon the point of his tail; and the condemnation which brought him to a horizontal position, was rather in his favour than against him. This story, in its nature, is too childish and trifling for serious remark. It is, however, a story which has found its way into other theological systems of great antiquity.

And the followers of Moses have to contend with many of the eastern nations, such as Egyptians, Persians, and Indians, upon the merit of originality. There is a similarity in almost all supernatural systems of theology; they are all founded in a disgusting distortion of nature; they are all interwoven with the "marvelous;" they have all their serpents, their ghosts, and their devils. It is not of importance who first invented these theological wonders; they are not the less foolish and injurious, whether they were first propagated by the followers of Moses, or the disciples of Zoroaster; whether they are of Egyptian or Indian origin. They are still the dreams of fanaticism, and have perverted all the pure ideas of God and Nature, which man otherwise would have formed.

Concerning the invention of the Devil, of good and bad spirits, with which all ancient theology is replete, there is, in Volney's "Ruins," a most striking passage, which throws much philosophic light upon the subject. "In Persia, it was the serpent which, under the name of Ahrimanes, formed the basis of the system of Zoroaster; and it is the same, Christians and

Jews, that is become your serpent of Eve; (the celestial origin) and that of the cross in both cases, the emblem of Satan, the great adversary of the ancient of days sung by Daniel. In Syria, it was the hog, or wild boar, enemy of Adonis; because in that country the office of the northern bear was made to devolve upon the animal whose fondness for mire and dirt emblematical of winter. And it is for this reason that you, children of Moses and Mahomet, hold this animal in abhorrence, in imitation of the priests of Memphis and Balbec, who detested him as the murderer of their god, the sun. This is likewise. O Indians! the type of your Chiben, which was once the Pluto of your brethren, the Greeks and Romans; your Brama also, (God the creator) is only the Persian Ormuzd, and the Osiris of Egypt, whose very name expresses a creative power, producer of forms. And these gods are worshiped in a manner analogous to the real or fictitious attributes; and the worship, on account of the difference of its objects, was divided into two distinct branches; in one, the benign God received a worship of joy and love, whence are derived all religious acts of a gay nature, festivals, dances, banquets, offerings of flowers, milk, honey, perfumes, in a word, of every thing that delights the senses and the soul. In the other, the malign, on the contrary, received a worship of fear and pain, whence originated all religious acts of the sombre kind, tears, grief, mourning, self-denial, blood-offerings, and cruel sacrifices. You now understand," continued the orator, addressing himself to the Indians, Persians, Jews, Christians, and Muslim, "you now understand the origin of those ideas of combats and rebellions, which equally pervade your respective mythology."

It is thus that this beautiful writer has developed the origin of these religious ideas; and it is in this manner that the disordered imagination has operated upon subjects that could not be reduced to certitude. There is not, however, perhaps one malignant character amongst all those which theology has created, who has acted a more conspicuous part than the Christian Devil, or Satan. He comes forth under this latter name in the book of Job, and there assumes to himself the right of keeping the best of company, and carrying on vast projects of ruin, mischief, and rascality. He introduces himself among the sons of God, and holds a familiar and social conversation with the Creator himself. God, according to the story, condescends to indulge him in this kind of intimacy, and they unite in forming a scheme to torment and ruin the unfortunate Job. The coalition and the project so effectually disgrace the character of the Deity, that no genuine Theist can read the story without emotions of disgust and resentment against its foolish fabricators. Satan is here put upon a par with God himself, and they mutually coalesce in a scheme to torment and destroy an upright and honest man. Such representations of God annihilate at once the validity of any book in which they are found. Another extraordinary story concerning the Devil is told in the New Testament, which describes him as having fallen into much worse company than he had been accustomed to keep, according to the accounts in the book of Job. There he was found among the sons of God; but in the latter case, amongst a herd of swine. This passage must be quoted, because it is worthy of comment; it shows how miserably inconsistent is the Christian system of religion; it shows the extent of fanatic credulity, and the impositions which priestcraft has laid upon uninstructed man.

"And there was a good way off from them an herd of many swine feeding. So the devils besought him, saying, if thou cast us out, suffer us to go away into the herd of swine. And he said unto them, go. And when they were come out, they went into the herd of swine; and behold the whole herd of swine ran violently down a steep place, and perished in the waters." (Matthew chap. viii.) It appears by this passage, that these devils had a desire to change their residence, which was granted to them, and they forthwith entered the swine, and took up their abode there; but it seems that these brute animals, by some unknown impulse, probably of a devilish kind, since it is clear that the Devil was in them, plunged into the water, and were instantly drowned. Now the morality and utility of the business must be settled by Christian theologists. Whether were the devils in this case drowned with the hogs, or did they make their escape the moment that they were immersed in water? If they really made their escape, there could be no use in sending them into the swine; and if they were actually drowned, then one might with truth assert, that the Devil is dead. In the fifth chapter of Mark, this same story is related, and it is said, that the swine, into which the devils entered, were about 2,000 in number, and that they all ran violently down a steep place, and were drowned in the sea. To have given this impulse to the whole herd, it is necessary that each one should have been possessed with a devil; it follows, therefore, that 2,000 devils must have been drowned, or, if they made their escape, that 2,000 hogs must have perished for no valuable purpose whatever.

In any view of the story it is is marked with injustice and inhumanity; injustice toward those who were the rightful owners of these swine, and inhumanity or cruelty toward the swine themselves. It is a tale of a childish nature; but it shows what strange conceptions theology has formed concerning devils, and many other airy phantoms. In another part of Matthew's gospel, the Devil is said to have taken Jesus up into a high mountain, for the purpose of tempting him, and offering him all the kingdoms of the earth for his homage and worship. This same Jesus, Christians believe to be God himself, or equal to God, and yet he condescends to be led about by the Devil, and holds with him a conversation. A book that exhibits such accounts, such dereliction of all dignity and correctness of conduct in the Creator, could never be written by a spirit of truth. The Devil is represented as being every where at the same time; ubiquity is one of his leading attributes, and he goeth about like a roaring lion seeking whom he may devour; he is omniscient as well as omnipresent, he knows every thing that is going on in heaven, earth, and hell, and is continually exerting his power to defeat the projects of his celestial competitor. Such is the description which Christian theology gives of that malignant Devil, which it has created to answer the purposes of interest and terror. This being is so essential to the clerical scheme and its advocates, that a certain writer observes, that they could not do without him. But it will perhaps be said, that the Devil has a powerful effect in restraining men from vice; his existence, combined with the idea of hell, is necessary to deter the multitude from the commission of enormous crimes.

In this point of view, the subject assumes a more serious character, and merits attention. An appeal to the nature of the case, and to facts, will furnish, in some measure, the satisfactory solution of any supposed difficulty upon the present subject. It is a well known truth, that an immediate and certain evil of a much less severe nature, of much less weight and magnitude, has much greater effect upon the human mind, than those that are distant and uncertain, even when their size and terrific appearance become extended in an infinite degree. Show to a man the certain and sudden consequences of an action; let his mind be strongly impressed with an idea that there is no escape from such fatal effect, and he will recoil with horror from the perpetration of a deed, which would bring along with it such a speedy ruin and excruciating misery. In the apprehension which relates to distant punishment, there is a great drawback upon its acuteness and severity, arising from the single consideration that it may never happen, or that intervening causes may diminish the malignity of its nature, or the fury of its operation. When, for instance, a man is about to take feloniously his neighbor's goods, he does not look behind him to see whether the Devil is watching his motions; no, but he keeps a vigilant eye upon the owner of the property, or the bystanders in general; if these can be evaded, the Devil is set at defiance. The account can be settled with him at a future day; but with the owner of the goods there can be no postponement of the business.

With the civil law, the settlement must be instant, and the compensation adequate and complete; there is a corporal, moral, and pecuniary punishment, which has a powerful effect in restraining man from vice, and without these, all the hells of fanaticism would never be able to hold him to the point of substantial virtue: he would fly off in a moral tangent, from the great circle of human happiness, and sow the seeds of disorder in the very bosom of society. Take away from man these restraints, justly imposed by the civil law; take away the love of reputation, which is a strong and active sentiment of the human heart; take away that internal idea of discrimination in the character of human actions; the idea that one class is useful and amiable, and that another is injurious and detestable; take from the constitution of man these powerful motives in the cause of virtue, and you will strip him of the most influential considerations by which he is bound to the faithful performance of his duty; let him loose under these circumstances, and neither the Devil, nor the fear of hell, would be sufficient to fasten his attention upon the practice of an exalted morality.

In support of this assertion, we may safely appeal to the evidence of facts. For many hundred years past the Christian religion, and its powerful advocates, the clergy, have combined to restrain a wicked world from acts of degrading and destructive criminality; they have portrayed the subject in all the frightful and impressive points of view, of which it was susceptible; they have represented hell with all its horrors, the Devil in all his malignity, and, combined with these, an angry God, not less terrific in his character; notwithstanding all this, these pious men are continually crying out that the world is growing worse and worse; that infidelity is increasing, and that we are treasuring up wrath against the day of wrath, and the righteous display of the awful vengeance of God. If such be the fact, these boasted restraints have not answered the purpose; if such be the fact, they might as well have been without a Devil, for he appears to have answered them no purpose. Men who do not believe in this immoral monster, are frequently more virtuous, and never more vicious, than many who declare that they would not for all the world renounce the belief of a Devil. Among those nations, where the reign of terror has been the most complete, there has been the least virtue, the least morality, the least attention to the rights and dignity of human nature. Spain, Portugal, and Italy, have been eminent for their attachment to the Christian religion; for their pious zeal and unshaken faith in the gospel, and yet there is scarcely a spot upon the globe where moral principle is less understood, or more universally abandoned in practice, than it is in these wretched and superstitious countries.

If the machinery of the Christian religion could have answered the purpose of moral restraint, a fair opportunity has been given among many Christian nations for proving, in this respect, the efficacy of this religion. It has not, however, been proved, and the fact is, that the most religious countries have been the most immoral. The horrors of the inquisition, the cruelties of Spain and other countries of Europe, upon the peaceable and unoffensive inhabitants of America, are not yet forgotten; they are still fresh in the mind, and evince with indubitable certainty, that the spirit of Christianity is ferocious cruelty, and not a generous and exalted benevolence toward the human race. Facts are therefore in pointed opposition to the opinion, that the terrific part of revealed religion has aided the cause of moral virtue. The condition of man in nature impels him to virtue; but superstition has perverted his heart, and deranged the operations of his understanding. It is the business and the duty of reason to restore him to intellectual sanity, to exalt the feelings of his heart, and give to his energies a new impulse productive of universal happiness.

CHAPTER XVII

Death, or the Disorganization of Intelligent Beings

Painful sensations are often the consequences of surveying the history of man. The means of ingenious torture are every where discovered, and the imagination gives an accumulating impulse to the development of their operations. The ingenuity and the fury of fanaticism are continually busied in manufacturing misery for unfortunate mortals. The natural and unavoidable evils which are connected with the condition of human life are not sufficient; the disordered fancy of man seeks in the distant heavens, or in futurity, the causes calculated to produce by anticipation, a new modification of distress; and, in this respect, enthusiasm has been extremely successful. It has awakened all the fears of weak and ignorant mortals, and taken special care to convert this to its own profit and advantage. Death, which is as natural as life, has been converted into a fruitful source of revenue, and clerical avarice has been satiated through the channel of human frailty and destruction. It is not sufficient that man is every where subjected to the natural and unavoidable influence of the elementary world; to pain, sickness, and inevitable calamities of every sort, without being alarmed by the terrors which superstition has connected with his ultimate dissolution. Must this final event of our temporary existence become the cause of perpetual torture during our life? Must the mind of man be for ever on the rack, in consequence of an anticipated evil, which no prudence or foresight can possibly prevent? Must the unpleasant sensations, which result from the capacity of our natures, be increased by the artificial ingenuities of a blind and fanatic zeal? Is there no source from whence to draw consolation and mental tranquility; no fundamental principles of repose and happiness; no primary objects, of delight, calculated to dissipate the mist of ignorance and general wretchedness? Yes, and they are to be found in the established order of nature. My object, therefore, in this chapter, is to reconcile man to his fate; to tranquillize his mind, and raise it above the superstitious fears of death; to call into action his fortitude and his reason, and by a justifiable exhibition of the general and uniform operation of the laws of nature, to increase the quantity of human happiness. To do this with success, it is necessary to destroy the prejudices and the evils which are connected with the belief of ancient systems.

It is universally agreed and verified by the experience of all past ages, that death is the inevitable fate of every sensitive and intelligent agent: but it is denied by philosophy, that this death is the consequence of any primary apostasy of the supposed first parents of the human race. But since a contrary belief has obtained throughout all the Christian world, it becomes our duty to make the necessary inquiry respecting this strange and unnatural doctrine, and develope the true causes of ultimate disorganization in the human species. In doing this, we shall examine the threefold death of the Christians. First, Spiritual Death. Secondly, Temporal Death. Thirdly, Eternal Death.

These three kinds of death have been foolishly attributed to the sin of Adam, when, in fact, the first and the last are not true, and neither of them bears any relation to the supposed violation of moral law. By spiritual death, Christians understand a total corruption and debasement of the moral qualities of our nature, by which man is rendered incapable of the performance of any virtuous action; and this, they say, has been the fatal consequence of the primitive defection of Adam, who violated the command of heaven, by eating of the forbidden fruit. Let us examine this doctrine on the principle of nature, reason, and justice.

The moral qualities of our nature are capable of being drawn into action, in perfect coincidence with the fundamental principles of an exalted virtue; but it is also conceded, that they are capable of being vitiated. In every intelligent agent, actions of the most opposite nature will sometimes obtain; man is not wholly virtuous, nor is he wholly vicious; but he consists of a compound of these two different kinds of action; but whether virtuous or vicious, it is the result of his own choice, and the use of the moral energies of his nature; his virtue is always personal, and his vices are to be attributed to a source which entitles them to a similar denomination. He acts as an independent moral agent; he acts for himself, he is accountable for himself, and "he" cannot be justifiably incriminated by the vices of another, neither can another be incriminated by "his" violation of moral rectitude. In this case, personal moral agency is the correct ground of decision, and to this tribunal alone the whole must be deferred.

From this statement it ought to be perceived, that the partial corruption of our natures and character is admitted through its proper channel; but it ought also to be evident, that no concession is made relative to a transfer of personal immorality. What, then, can these spiritual doctors mean, when they speak of a spiritual death referable to the primary apostasy of Adam? Do they mean that these personal infractions of moral law are to be attributed to the conduct of him who lived six thousand years ago? Do they mean to exhibit the idea of a double incrimination, in consequence of one present and personal infraction? Do they mean to charge "Adam" with the sins of the whole world, and afterward each individual with "his" portion of the national debt of iniquity? Would they procure two judgments, two payments, and then remain unsatisfied? Yes, "and after all, the whole debt must be eventually canceled by the death and sufferings of Jesus Christ."

Christians, can you examine seriously the nature of human actions, and still contend for the propriety of such unnatural doctrines? Will you never give to man his due degree of merit, and reward him for his real virtue. Is there nothing tender, nothing sympathetic, nothing moral in the heart of an intelligent being? Is there no justice for the benefit of society, no benevolence to brighten the character of man, no humanity for the relief of distressed objects? Is the heart wholly corrupted, and the mental qualities of our nature totally vitiated? Are there no principles preserved in operation, honorable to the character of the human species? It is in vain to attempt, at this enlightened day, to impose a religion upon the world, which tortures all the social faculties of our nature, and reduces man to the condition of a brute; it is in vain to say there is no moral goodness, no elevated sentiments of virtue, no beneficial operations of the heart, by which to preserve the happiness of the human species. Society could never exist without the influence of moral principles, and the practice of real virtue; but since it both exists and proceeds in a manner mutually beneficial to all its members, it is fair to conclude, that its preservation is to be ascribed to the exercise of a social morality, and this morality fundamentally connected with the nature and condition of man.

But admitting for a moment that the world is as vicious as it has been represented, it does not follow that this aggregate of wickedness is to be attributed to the sin of Adam; but the contrary is evident from the personal nature of moral actions, and the responsibility connected with the character of intelligent beings. Let fanaticism and superstition therefore exhibit their labored discourses on this supposed spiritual death; they speak of phantoms and not of realities, they lose sight of the moral nature of man, and the sources of human action; virtue and vice are confounded and their transferable nature serves only to perplex the understanding, and destroy the line of personal and discriminative justice. This spiritual death may serve to augment the mysteries and follies of the Christian religion; but I am confident it will never serve the cause of virtue, or lead to the practice of genuine morality. I proceed to the consideration of temporal death.

This temporal death, which is the death that every man suffers when he leaves the theater of human action, seems to be less mysterious and more cognizable by the human mind; we are taught the knowledge of it by the experience of all ages and all countries; by our own observation on the facts and events constantly presented to our contemplation. Death is the inevitable portion of every living creature; it is the certain fate of every organized being; it is the counterpart of our original construction; it is a change in the mode of existence; it is a dissolution of the combined modifications of animal life; it is a physical property of every sensitive agent; it is the eternal mutability of infinitely diversified modes of being; it is established in the primary arrangements of Nature; it is a property, and ever will be, of the parts of all existence. Death is as natural and as necessary as life; the preservation of the latter is an unavoidable effect of the former. Change or mutability is essentially connected with the uniform harmony and preservation of the great fabric of the universe; and no one can expect to be excepted from the operation of this general law. Vice is not the cause, though it may accelerate the event; the seeds of death are contained in the original organizations of our natures; sensation and reflection by their necessary operation lead to decay. Life is naturally progressive to a certain point, which, having passed, it necessarily retrogrades toward a state of dissolution. This is the true condition, the just and eternal order of organized existence, and the knowledge of this ought to be the highest consolation of a reflecting mind. But here, Superstition, from her dismal and dark recess, cries out heresy, and proclaims damnation to the man who dares to reason on the ground of nature; we hear her awful voice sounding hollow in her dark and gloomy abodes, and we regard it not. Reason whispers in our ear and says, "Pursue with indefatigable zeal the cause of Nature, develop truth, and labor for the happiness of the human race."

But after all, how is it possible we can attribute temporal death to the sin of Adam? Did this transgression change the physical organization of man? Did it destroy any of his natural faculties, or make an addition to those he was already possessed of? If so, what was the construction of Adam previous to his supposed fall from a state of innocence? If he was possessed of sensation, he must have been exposed to pain; if he was exposed to pain, he was liable to death, for death is often the consequence of severity of pain; if he was not possessed of sensation, he must have been a being entirely different from ourselves, and consequently could not have been the parent of the human race. It follows, therefore, that there is no point of view in which this subject can be considered, which will warrant the conclusion, that death is to be attributed to the primitive apostasy of Adam. It follows, both physically and morally, it is unjust. Some other cause of corporeal dissolution should, therefore, be discovered, and this, as we have seen, is to be found in our natural texture and arrangement. The next principle of discussion is what is called eternal death, or a state of endless punishment.

This kind of death cannot be the consequence either of Adam's transgression, or the aggregate wickedness of the whole human race. It is an idea which has been generated in the brain of fanaticism, and supported by the enthusiastic zeal of persecuting superstition. It was not sufficient to subject mankind to the terrible effects of total moral turpitude, and temporal disorganization; but the fury of religious malignity has been exerted to invent a new species of torture to endure for endless ages. In the invention and establishment of this doctrine, the nature of human actions and the principles of justice have been entirely disregarded. To verify this assertion, it is only necessary to examine the qualities of human actions, and the crimes which are supposed to merit this terrible infliction of punishment.

Man is a being possessed of certain powers and faculties; of certain passions and propensities to actions, and these, by a primary law of nature, are subjected to control of reason, and are to be directed by conscience, or an internal moral sense of right and wrong. But what are these faculties, what are these passions which are essentially connected with the character and condition of intelligent agents? Our existence and all the properties of it are of a limited and finite nature; there is not one single quality of man that is not imperfect; the parts of the aggregate of his life do not constitute any thing like infinity. In all his movements, in all his energies, in all the capacities of his being, he is regulated by finite and not by infinite principles. He is incapable of any actions which do not result essentially from the faculties which he is possessed of; all his conduct must have a strict reference to the causes which have produced it, and every effect must bear a proportion to its productive cause. If the cause be limited and imperfect, the effect must also be imperfect, for the effect can never rise superior to the cause which has given it birth.

Before we speak, therefore, of an infinite sin, or an infinite evil, we should consider the capacity of those beings to whom this evil is attributed; if the acting agents are infinite in their nature and character, the effects of their operations may be so too, but if they are finite, their actions can lay no claim to an infinite effect. Sin is the consequence of the infraction of moral law; if this infraction be made by an infinite being, the criminality would be like the being who made it, that is of an infinite quality; but if the infraction be made by an imperfect being, the criminality is finite, and limited in its essential nature. It follows, of course, as man is a finite and imperfect agent; if he cannot do an infinite act, he is incapable of an infinite evil, and does not deserve an infinite punishment; consequently, the idea of eternal death is unjust and unreasonable.

But further, if every sin were an infinite evil, which is the Christian doctrine, it would merit an infinite punishment; but if one sin deserves an infinite punishment, what must be the punishment of him who is guilty of ten thousand sins? According to this doctrine he must be liable to ten thousand infinite punishments, which is a physical and moral absurdity. This doctrine of eternal death or infinite punishment, disregards the nature of human actions, and every principle of distributive justice. It inflicts on the smallest offender as great extent and severity of punishment as on the most abandoned criminal. It goes to the destruction of all moral virtue, by inducing man to believe, that the commission of one vicious action is as odious in the sight of God, and deserves as much punishment as a thousand violations of moral rectitude. It destroys all relation between the actions of men and the beneficial arrangements of corrective improvement. It makes man infinite, and the Deity unjust; both of which are inconsistent with the nature of things and the principles of eternal truth.

It is impossible that there should be more than one infinite being in existence, and this being is the God of nature, the intelligent organizer of the universe; possessed of all possible perfection and excellence, and directing the vast concerns of nature with the greatest harmony, and the most divine benevolence. This being is incapable of any infraction of moral law, and this excludes from the system of nature, the possibility of an infinite evil, and consequently the justice of an infinite punishment is also excluded, and with it the principle of eternal death. Thus the belief of an eternal Hell is essentially erroneous, and can claim no justifiable foundation in Nature or Nature's God. This doctrine of endless punishment tortures the whole system of distributive justice; is pernicious to the well-being of society; is virtually destructive of the moral energies of man, and degrades the dignity and perfections of the divine Creator of the universe.

The Christian doctrine of death, spiritual, temporal, and eternal, has now been considered, and the whole proved to bear no relation to the sin of Adam, or the primitive apostasy of the reputed parents of the human race. It has been shown that spiritual death is nothing more than a partial corruption of the moral qualities of our nature, and even this partial corruption has resulted from personal violation of moral law. It has been shown also, that temporal death is the physical property of our existence, and has been unphilosophically attributed to the sin of Adam. It has also been proved, that eternal death or endless punishment, is inconsistent with the nature of human actions, and the qualities and properties of finite agents. In short, the Christian idea of death is inconsistent with reason, bears no affinity to truth or nature, and violates the primitive order of the world established by God himself. Some observations, therefore, deduced from the reason and nature of things, shall conclude this chapter.

In examining the vast machinery of the universe, presented for our contemplation by the great Creator, the human mind is lost in a labyrinth of reflection, and swallowed up in the most profound meditations! We behold on every side the most ineffable beauties and the most astonishing wonders; the most splendid exhibitions of eternal wisdom, the most unbounded displays of infinite benevolence, and the most perfect testimonies of an incomprehensible power. In this vast system, there are many things inexplicable to man; many events beyond the power of human solution, and many arrangements incomprehensible by the most scrutinizing efforts of human wisdom. But man should consider himself as a unit in the totality of existence; as a part of a widely extended whole, bearing a relation to every other part, and every other part bearing a relation to his own modification of life. He should reflect that the world is governed by general and immutable laws, and that the immutable operation of these laws produces perpetual mutability in the infinitely diversified parts and portions of the great fabric of nature. He ought to learn that change is the eternal order in the established arrangements of the world, and he ought not to expect to be excluded from the general influence of fundamental laws established by eternal wisdom. He should learn to be reconciled to his fate, and consider death as a necessary and justifiable appendage of the present modification of existence. He should be taught to love and practice virtue, but not through the fear of an eternal hell; but because it is useful to society, and contributes to his individual happiness. He should be taught to revere the power which animates and enlivens the great system of nature; but not to fear God on the one hand, nor flatter him on the other, with an expectation of obtaining his favour. He should disregard all ideas of ghosts, demons, and malignant spirits, and reason on the cognizable properties of real existence. The mind of man should be elevated above the practice of vice, above the frowns of fortune, and the fears of death. He ought to be the strong advocate of nature, "and have confidence in his own energies;" his principles should be just and correct, his actions strictly moral, and his sentiment in coincidence with the system of benevolence and utility. No bugbears of superstition, no ghosts of fanaticism, no demons of hell should be permitted to disturb his brain; but, rising above all vice and all prejudice, he should consider himself as an associated being, and live for the benefit of himself and his fellow creatures.

CHAPTER XVIII

Proposition, That the Want of Universality of the Christian Religion Demonstrates that It is Not of Divine Origin

E very production must of necessity bear a strict relation to its cause. If the cause be imperfect, it is to be expected that the production will exhibit some strong feature of imperfection. If, on the contrary, the cause be perfect, the effect will carry along with it the unequivocal proofs of that perfection. If these assertions be applied to a system of religion, it would not be difficult to ascertain the source and origin of such religion. A religion, therefore, claiming divine origin, ought, by the nature of its doctrines and principles, to produce conviction in the mind, that it is really supernatural and divine. It ought to exhibit the proof of this celestial birth in so clear and striking a manner, as to be capable of being embraced by every capacity interested in a knowledge of its nature and consequences.

It is unreasonable and unjust in the advocates of any system to announce divinity of origin where the internal evidence derived from the scheme itself is sufficient to demonstrate imperfection. A supernatural code of theological principles should be incapable of being charged with any of those defects which are unavoidably connected with all human productions; contradictions, inconsistencies, and immorality, can never be found in the mandates of a being infinitely perfect; infinite perfection precludes the possibility of such effect, and wherever the defect is discovered, the evidence growing out of such defect is abundant against the admission of divine origin. Keeping these principles constantly in view, as marks by which to direct our inquiries, we shall be able to ascertain what degree of respect we ought to bestow upon a system of theology, which has heretofore demanded the unqualified credence of every living creature to whom it has been presented; we shall be able to ascertain whether ignorance, superstition, and a fanatic zeal, have had any share of influence in producing the marvelous attachment which the votaries of every unnatural religion have inconsiderately bestowed upon the mysterious doctrines therein contained. It is with difficulty, amidst the prejudices that assail us, that the mind has recourse to the fundamental principles of truth, and the immutable laws from which it results; but we should learn to dismiss our unreasonable attachments, and exercise affection toward those principles only which are sanctioned by the voice of reason, and which bear a constant relation to the order of the physical world. Man is essentially interested in the discovery of truth, and the diversified application of its principles to all the concerns of human life; he is equally interested in the practice of a pure natural virtue; truth, however, will make but little progress, where religious bigotry has seized upon the mental faculties, and suppressed the elevated conception of the understanding; nor will practical virtue share a better fate, where its beneficent effects are opposed by similar causes; the hope, therefore, of constituting a useful character, compounded of the love of truth, and the practice of genuine morality, will become evanescent, unless man can be persuaded that he is interested in a speedy return to nature, from which, in all his inquiries, he has so long deviated. The plan of revealed religion, in which man for so many ages has reposed the confidence of his mind, should be re-examined under the impressions inducing an invincible attachment to the development of solemn truth, and the diffusion of general felicity; and it is with sentiments of this kind that we proceed to the examination of the subject proposed. If the Christian religion be true, we are essentially interested in a knowledge of this truth; if it be false, our happiness must be increased by a disclosure of those proofs which invalidate its authenticity. It is presumed, that forcible evidence can be adduced from the partiality of the scheme itself. This religion, destined to enlighten mankind, and lead them to the possession of sublime happiness, has, by its supposed author, been concealed from a considerable part of those very beings who must all be equally interested in the knowledge and the application of its doctrines. The assertion will not be controverted by any Christian advocates, who have any tolerable portion of geographical information.

It is in strict conformity with truth to say, that two-thirds of mankind, and perhaps three-fourths of them, are destitute of any knowledge of the Christian religion; and to verify this assertion, the learned geographer must indulge us while we take a short view of the situation of the globe in this respect. In America, it is true, that the Christian religion has been disseminated among all its civilized inhabitants; but there is a large portion of an opposite description, that have not been thus highly favored by the Divinity. Almost all the aborigines of this country are entirely destitute of any knowledge of supernatural religion; they grovel in their native darkness, abandoned in this respect "by the divine power that produced them," and left to form a variety of conjectures relative to a subject so essentially interesting to their present and their future welfare. In traveling to the old world, and including the aggregate of population, the feelings of the Christian heart will not be better consoled. Europe, it is true, with some trifling exceptions, may be considered as nominally Christian, but in going eastward, and entering the vast regions of the Asiatic world, we there behold 500,000,000 of inhabitants, which is more than half the human race, totally deprived of every information concerning this holy religion, deemed by its advocates essential to the felicity of intelligent beings. The exceptions in this part of the globe are too inconsiderable to engage our attention in this general calculation. Here the number of proselytes might have been somewhat greater, had not the conduct of the Christian missionaries laid the foundation of their expulsion for ever. In Africa, the remaining quarter of the globe, our inquiries will terminate in a discovery of the same ignorance relative to revealed religion. The exceptions here are as inconsiderable as those already noticed in regard to Asia. For the truth of these assertions an appeal is made to the best information of the civilized world.

The application of these facts to the subject under consideration, will operate essentially against the benevolence of that being, who is said to be the author and promulgator of this religion. It will be necessary, on the one hand, for the advocates of revelation to abandon the idea of its universal necessity, and the consideration that it is the sole cause of procuring felicity: or, on the other, to acknowledge that the God they worship is a partial, cruel, and vindictive parent, depriving his creatures of necessary information, and consigning them to future destruction for involuntary ignorance. It is a maxim of this celestial religion, that he that believeth not shall be damned; but how is man to believe a proposition of which he has no knowledge? How can he embrace a religion which he has never heard of? And, above all, how can criminality be attached by a just God to a want of belief, where no opportunity has been afforded of bestowing an assent? Are not all the human race equally the children of one common and benevolent parent? Are they not all fed by his bounty, and supported by his universal beneficence? Do they not all experience the benefits resulting from that luminous body, which in turn enlightens and fructifies the earth? Whence then this unjust discrimination, this partial arrangement in the moral concerns of man? But the advocates of the Christian religion will perhaps retort and say, "Do you believe that God is the author of the system of nature?" Yes. "Do you contend that he has been impartial, and that he has bestowed equal talents and faculties on all?" No. "Why, then, if you admit partiality in one case, do you complain of it in another?" The objection is plausible, and deserves an answer.

In doing this it is to be remarked, that there is an essential difference in the nature of the two cases. In the case of the Christian religion, man is subjected to damnation, either because he is ignorant of the system, or because his mind cannot discern the quantum of evidence necessary to establish its divine origin; but in the system of nature, although there is a real difference in regard to the possession of talents, yet the man weak in intellect cannot, in justice, be subjected to punishment on this account. No Christian will contend that great mental energy will entitle a man to salvation, or, on the other hand, that a feeble understanding will, in the mind of the Deity, be considered as a justifiable cause of damnation. No; if God be just, he will require only the due and proper exercise of those diversified talents which he had variously bestowed upon his creatures. If one be weak and another strong, one foolish and another discerning, the justice of God demands a mode of treatment exactly adjusted to these different powers and faculties. The Christian religion, therefore, in order to accord with the system of nature, should have annexed no penalty to unbelief, whether that belief resulted from total ignorance, or an honest dissent of mind, after a due examination of the evidence. The evidence of any system of religion ought to be equal to all, where equal credence is demanded of all. By what rules of moral justice does the Deity demand the unqualified belief of the present generation upon a less degree of evidence than he is said to have formerly exhibited? If miracles be necessary in one age to establish the truth of Christianity, they are equally necessary in every age. If one country be favoured with supernatural proofs, all other countries are equally entitled to the same unequivocal, convincing, and demonstrative testimony. If impartiality be considered as an attribute of God, this impartiality should at all times and in all places be preserved with an undeviating uniformity; but in every case where merit is attributed to the human assent, on the ground of supernatural proof, and in every other case where demerit is attached to unbelief, when the evidence in quantity and quality is of an inferior nature, this principle is notoriously abandoned.

Again, if the Christian religion be true, the proofs ought

not only to be universally exhibited, but they ought also to be universally convincing; and this results essentially from the nature of that evidence which is employed to substantiate the system. It is not strange that man should often doubt, where human testimony is the only ground of conviction, but when the proof rises higher and claims a divine origin, one would suppose that the mind must necessarily yield to the force of such divine testimony, otherwise the means made use of by divine power for the accomplishment of the end, are inadequate and deficient; but as no such imbecility can justly be attributed to a being possessing infinite wisdom, it is to be presumed, that the exhibition of evidence in the present case ought to be complete and satisfactory, universal and every where convincing. If human projects miscarry, this failure is to be ascribed to the imperfection of human nature; and the believer ought to perceive that he does virtually ascribe to his God the same kind of imperfection, whenever he acknowledges a defeat in the completion of any object, the producing of which was deemed important in the mind of the Supreme Being. It were less pernicious for man to believe in no God, than to believe in one that is wicked and imperfect, partial and vindictive, establishing his systems upon no principle of distributive justice, and acting upon principles neither correct, beneficial, nor universally understood. Those immoral monsters to whom men in all ages have paid adoration, have served only to corrupt the morality of the human heart, and exhibit examples destructive to the cause of virtue. Such, however, is the character of all those beings who have been made the authors of supernatural schemes of religion. It is time that man should abandon his errors, and return to nature; it is time that he should elevate his conceptions above the prejudices resulting from a partial religion, and attribute to the benevolent parent of universal existence, those attributes only which can possibly adorn his character. The barbarous divinity of the Christian religion has marked all his arrangements with a partiality and vindictive cruelty, which strip him of every amiable property, and subject the mind to the terrific impressions which naturally flow from anger and revenge. When believers shall prove their God to be just and impartial, they may solicit with confidence the gratitude of the human heart; but the rational mind beholds in the arrangements of supernatural religion the most unequivocal injustice, and the abandonment of every principle by which the preserver of nature ought ever to be influenced. Show us a religion universally promulgated and universally proved, and man will soon discover both its truth and utility, and that its revelation is worthy of the being whom he adores. This religion is the religion of nature, it is the practice of justice, it consists in acts of extensive beneficence, it is not confined to any age or country, it is established over the face of the whole earth, it is complete and universal, it is comprehensible by every mind, it is useful to every creature, it is the indestructible cement of intelligent nature in every part of the universe.

CHAPTER XIX

That Moral Principles are Not Founded upon Theological Ideas, Nor upon any Sectarian Modification of these Ideas, but Upon a Basis as Immortal and Indestructible as Human Existence Itself

The different religious sectaries, which have prevailed in the world, have furnished innumerable proofs of the bigoted tenacity so strikingly characteristic of supernatural theology. It is not only in regard to their doctrines that this disposition has appeared, but each sect has laid claim to a preeminent preservation of morals, and to the power of rendering good and happy a wicked and apostate race of men. The fulminating anathemas of the Church have been poured forth in every direction, and the most petty sectary has raised around itself a rampart for the alternate purpose of self-defense, and attack upon heretics and unbelievers. They have universally charged each other with holding doctrines of a demoralizing nature, and subversive of the moral purity of rational existence. In such a state of things reason owes to the happiness of man the faithful discharge of an important duty, consisting of a candid and temperate investigation concerning theological ideas, and the foundation of moral principles. Reason has indulged an opinion that virtue rests upon a more stable basis, than the sectarian theology of past ages, and that the aggregate number of sectaries have been altercating superficially the reciprocal relation which their respective doctrines bear to each other; that they have abandoned the ground of substantial support, which nature has given to the principles of a pure and incorruptible morality, and that their acrimonious strictures and recriminations have served only to perplex the mind and vitiate the heart. The Jewish, the Christian, and the Mahometan theology furnishes the most incontrovertible facts, and presents the most convincing evidence respecting an ultimate decision of the present subject. But the internal and essential character of the inquiry first merits attention, before the collateral and subsequent consideration of sectarianism can lay any just claim to a share of influence in the final determination.

The mind of man, in every age of the world, has given diversified specimens of its ideas concerning supernatural powers. The physical universe is a grand and impressive spectacle, whose phenomena alarmed the terror-struck beholder, generating at one and the same time a thousand hopes and fears in the agitated and uninstructed intellect of man. The physical world was the grand reservoir.

It was the common source of Theological eductions, and every species of fanaticism drew from this fountain beings of such form and character as would best answer the various purposes for which they were intended. The characteristic differences and the moral or immoral shades of each deified object, were regulated by a thousand different causes existing in the passions and properties of intelligent life. The aggregate of nature was a terrible spectacle in the view of ignorance, and the parts of this grand whole being necessarily subjected to a more scrutinizing inspection of intellect, were discovered to be capable of producing various conjectures concerning spiritual substances and concealed agents of a benevolent or malignant kind. Various moral effects will no doubt be produced by the generation of so many spiritual monsters; but the effects produced upon moral practices are one thing, and the substantial basis of moral principle is another; they are quite different in their essential characters.

It is an old maxim, that evil communications corrupt good manners; and although corrupt associations, even with the pretext that one party is of celestial birth and character, will produce pernicious consequences, yet these are considerations separate and distinct from the true foundation of those immortal principles of virtue, by which the life of man ought to be governed. If a thousand Gods existed, or if nature existed independent of any, the moral relation between man and man would remain exactly the same in either case. Moral principle is the result of this relation, it is founded in the properties of our nature, and it is as indestructible as the basis on which it rests.

If we could abandon, for a moment, every theistical idea, it would nevertheless remain substantially true, that the happiness of society must depend upon the exercise of equal and reciprocal justice. It would also be true, that benevolence is an amiable trait in the character of man; that the cultivation of his faculties is a duty imposed on him, because the faithful performance of his duty extends the circle of his real felicity; that vice is the bane

of individual and social existence; that truth is to be preferred
to falsehood, activity to indolence, temperance to debauchery,
and, generally, that science and virtue claim pre-eminently over
ignorance and vice, the universal attachment of the human race.
All these, and many other particulars of a like nature, would
stand as immortal monuments of the real nature of moral principles, even after cultivated intellect shall have performed the
last solemn act of duty relative to the ancient regimen, and shall
have recalled bewildered man to the happy contemplation of
the laws and immutable energies of the physical universe.

If this be true, in regard to the essential nature of theological ideas, how much more powerfully will it hold upon
every sectarian modification of the subject. If pure theism
be independent of morality, and morality independent of
that, because it rests upon the relations and the properties of
human life, then it will be easy to conceive that the subordinate
descriptions of sectarian theology must be still more unconnected with the present subject. The character, however, of all
the gods of antiquity, is, of itself, a sufficient consideration to
exclude them from any participation in the concerns of an
exalted virtue. The Jewish God commands theft and murder;
he puts a lying spirit into the mouth of his prophets; he repents
and grieves for his past conduct; he is a God of fury, wrath,
and vengeance. These actions and qualities are all attributed
to him in the Old Testament! Is it possible that any man of
common sense can believe, that moral principles which are
so important to the best interests of human society, should be
placed upon such an immoral and vindictive foundation? Can
any one imagine that a being, so destitute of moral justice and
benevolence himself, could serve as a solid basis on which to
rest these qualities in human nature? No, this sectarian God,

this malignant phantom of former ages, this compound of weakness and wickedness, is calculated to subvert all moral principle, both in theory and practice, and present the moral world in the full exercise of the most detestable passions.

The wrathful and unrelenting character of the Christian divinity, is not less hostile to the immaculate principles of a sound and excellent morality; embittered in anger, and infuriate in his vengeance, he lays his hand upon his innocent Son, and offers him up a living sacrifice for the purposes which reason abhors, and justice utterly disclaims. Under the modification, name, and character of the Holy Ghost, this being introduces himself to a woman, and violates those correct and delicate sentiments which ought to guide an intelligent being in cases of this kind. Under the name and character of Jesus Christ, he exhibits the most flagrant departures from the purity of moral sentiment and moral practice. In proof of this, the reader is referred to the 9th chapter of this work.

The sectarian divinity, which Christianity presents to us, is represented as a consuming fire, as a being possessing fiery indignation and an uncontrollable vengeance; as a being who disregards all just discrimination upon the subject of moral principle. He declares in some parts of the New Testament, that every thing shall be regulated by his arbitrary will without regard to the nature or character of the case. "He will have mercy on whom he will have mercy, and whom he will he hardeneth." (See Rom. chap. ix. &c.) Is it possible that even a Christian believer can suppose, for a single moment, that the principles of genuine morality can rest upon such an arbitrary basis? No; a divinity of immoral description is the bane of moral virtue. The purest theism is independent of morality, and morality is independent of that; much less then can the corrupt and vitiated conceptions of barbarous ages be produced in support of a principle which could not exist without the intellectual faculties of man and which cannot be destroyed while these faculties exist. The principle and the practice of immortal virtue will long remain, after the plundering and bloody theology of Moses, Jesus, and Mahomet, has ceased to afflict the human race. The essential principles of morality are founded in the nature of man, they cannot be annihilated, they are as indestructible as human existence itself.

CHAPTER XX

Universal Benevolence

The sentiment which includes the whole sensitive and intelligent world, within the sphere of its benignant operations, is justly denominated universal benevolence. Every organized being, whether of a high or low station in animal existence, is susceptible of pleasure and pain; they are all alternately affected by the wishes, the passions, and the conduct of each other, and this influence is extended much further than at first view would strike the mind of the most correct and accurate observer. The universe is a vast assemblage of living creatures, whose relations are reciprocal and reciprocated under a thousand different forms, and supported by a thousand different ligaments of an imperceptible nature. The parts are interested in the whole, and the whole is interested in the preservation and diversified modification of the parts. Nothing is foreign or irrelevant in the vast fabric to which we belong. Union is most intimate, and the intellectual destiny which awaits the human race will ultimately disclose the consoling secret, that man's highest happiness consists in perspicuously discovering his true connection with nature, and the eternal duration of this connection. The circumscribed condition of man's existence, his wants, his social duties, his appetites, and his passions, constitute a considerable drawback upon the comprehensive conceptions, which he would otherwise have been capable of forming concerning his relationship with nature, and the ultimate destination to which the powers of nature have devoted the component and immortal parts of his existence. The intellectual properties of man are, however, capable of being expanded so far as to indulge an opinion subversive of those narrow views, which have excited sentiments of hostility between individuals and nations whose interests were the same, and whose duties ought to have been universally reciprocated.

It is, no doubt, extremely natural, and even absolutely necessary, that each individual should feel an anxiety extremely impulsive respecting the preservation of his own existence, and the means by which it is to be rendered tranquil and comfortable; but this sensation, the first which is experienced by a sensitive creature, does not preclude that expansion of mind which would benevolently extend the circle of man's moral affections and duties, and which also prepares for himself an additional portion of exalted enjoyment. Sensation alone, or, in other words, mere animal existence, must be deprived in a high degree of the power and the pleasure of reciprocating those sentiments of moral sympathy, to which intelligent man is indebted for his highest happiness. The gradual increase of the capacity of sensation constitutes a continual approach toward the possession of those properties on which the sublimity of thought depends, and by which human reason recognizes the benefit of benevolent reciprocation. It is, however, denied by some, that man possesses any other qualities than those which are merely selfish or individual; that his sensual impulses repel every sentiment of comprehensive kindness and affection; that in every respect he is a being of insulated nature and character, and that the powers and properties of his existence are necessarily in a high degree hostile to the interest and well-being of others.

Two points of prominent and conspicuous importance invite the activity of mind in the solution of the present difficulty. The one point is the physical relation of man to all existence: the other is his moral relation to his own species and to all other inferior animals. The component parts of which man is formed are all drawn from the great fountain of existence; they are essentially material in their nature, and destined to return to the source from which they sprang. Organized matter cannot lay claim to a pre-eminent essence; it is modification and refinement which produces visible exaltation, and not the native properties contained in the substance of which man is composed. The constant interchange of matter with matter, is a primary and immutable law of nature, and should teach man through the channel of observation the ultimate destiny that awaits him, it should teach him that the pain which he inflicts upon sensitive existence will return upon himself with interest, and will pave the way for eternizing a system of misery, fatal to the sensations of the whole animal world.

Humanity has lessons of a different kind, pregnant with salutary instructions, calculated to enforce conviction upon the intellectual powers of man. The spiritualization of human existence has made man a fool, it has taught him to spurn at matter, to contemn its power and ridicule its essence; whereas, on the contrary, sound philosophy, which unfolds the connection between man and nature, is calculated to produce in the mind sentiments of respect and tranquility; respect for the aggregate of existence to which he belongs, and tranquility at the idea of an eternal interest in this indestructible mass. The successive changes through which he is destined to pass, and the impossibility of relinquishing his connection with nature, should inspire him with feelings of universal sympathy, with sentiments of universal benevolence. Human reason has an important duty to perform in the institutions which it establishes; for these institutions will effect in succession all the portions of matter destined to pass through an organized predicament.

It is, no doubt, difficult to convince the human understanding of this physical or universal connection, or to make man see his true interest in this respect. It is, nevertheless, a solemn and philosophic truth that our sensations are, at this moment, suffering under the cruel lash of ancient institutions; that the whole animal world are reciprocating with each other a system of extensive and perpetual wretchedness, resulting principally from the contempt which has been thrown upon the capacity of material substance, and our ignorance of an important and an indestructible connection with the great body of nature. If man had a comprehensive view of the successive changes of his existence, and a correct idea of the nature of sensation continually resulting from the renovation of organic forms, sympathy or universal benevolence would become irresistibly impressive upon his moral powers, and form the basis of his subsequent conduct.

In the second place, man's moral relation to his own species, and to all other inferior animals, furnishes cogent evidence in favor of moral sympathy or universal benevolence. If the subject of man's physical connection presents us with some philosophical difficulties, the repeated and frequent necessity of performing his moral duties will furnish a mass of instruction adequate to every important decision. The single idea of establishing the doctrine of perpetual reprisals, ought to constitute an ample refutation of those selfish opinions which regard only the individual, to the exclusion of all the other members of society. It is the interest as well as the duty of every man to be just and benevolent; an opposite conduct would become the signal of universal discord, and the selfish principle, which at first had for its object the preservation of self, would become the procuring cause of self destruction.

The powers and the properties of human existence are of a similar nature, and require a correspondent method of treatment; beside, the intimate connection which subsists between us in this respect, our enjoyments and our capacity of enjoying, are augmented by every effort which the mind makes in a comprehensive system of philanthropy. The narrow prejudice which makes one man the enemy of another and one country the enemy of another, is not only disgraceful, but subversive of the best interests of human society. Political governments, and the prejudices which have been created and nurtured by these governments, have set individuals and nations in battle array against each other, without any good or substantial reason whatever. What is there in the nature of the case which should make a Frenchman and an Englishman hostile to each other? Are they not both men, possessed of similar faculties, equally indebted to nature for the resources of their felicity, and capable of being made happy or miserable by the operation of the same causes? Yes, and it is the iniquity of corrupt government which has perverted those sentiments of the human heart, by which one human being is bound to another in a general system of interest, sympathy, and universal benevolence.

This principle should also be extended to the whole animal world, so as to exclude acts of cruelty, and annihilate every species of injustice. The child that is permitted in early life to run a pin through a fly, is already half prepared to run dagger through the heart of his fellow creature! It is the duty of parents and the business of instruction, to correct the ferocious errors of former ages, and inspire society with sentiments of sympathy and universal goodness. But to do this with effect, our political institutions must be changed, and placed upon the broad basis of universal liberty and universal justice. This would be a work of time, but it is as certain in the ultimate issue of things, as the progress of the earth around the sun, or the general revolution of the planetary system. The individual that withholds his intellectual contribution in this respect, is either grossly ignorant, or a wicked traitor in the great cause of human existence.

CHAPTER XXI

Moses, Jesus, and Mahomet

The causes which have produced personal celebrity are numerous, and diversified by a thousand indescribable shades in their modes of operation. It also sometimes happens that the means of popular exaltation and perpetual fame have been either of a passive or uncontrollable nature. Such is the fact in the present case. Moses and Mahomet were active villains, whose characters cannot be examined without horror and detestation. They were both eminent murderers, and their debaucheries have been signalized by acts of barbarous brutality, of which the love-struck Solomon seems to be more destitute. The military ferocities and immoral decrees of these two "celestial" impostors have placed upon their characters an indelible stain, which the pretended sanctity of the priesthood can never wipe away!

Believers in Christianity, in reading the history and conduct of Moses, ought to blush for his crimes, and spurn at his blasphemy in attributing these crimes to the God whom he pretended to adore. He issues orders for the indiscriminate

massacre of men, women, and children, in a defenseless condition, making an exception only of that part of the captives
whose sexual predicament invited the passions of man to
indulge in the gratification of criminal desires. (See Numbers
chap. xxxi. verse 18, &c.)

But this is only a single specimen of the murdering temper of this meek man of God! From the time that he murdered the Egyptian and hid him in the sand, till the moment in
which he expired, and was buried without any man knowing
where he was buried, he exhibited examples of legerdemain
tricks, pretended familiarities with God, scenes of debauchery and malignant slaughter of the human race, which would
disgrace the most cruel despot of ancient or modern times.
For the truth of this remark an appeal is made to the historic
details contained in the books of Exodus, Numbers, and
Deuteronomy.

To show fully the immoral character of Moses, it would
be necessary to quote almost every chapter in these "holy
and inspired" books. Believers in revealed religion, who still
believe that Moses was a pious and meek man, ought, once
more, to pass in review the conduct and transactions which
the Bible has attributed to him: especially those details which
are contained in the books already mentioned. If there be any
member of the Christian church who can believe that God and
Moses ever united in the execution of those barbarous decrees
and immoral sentiments stated in these books, he must be lost
to all clear ideas of justice, and must have abandoned every
principle of humanity by which the life of man is to be rendered comfortable and happy. The author of "The Age of Reason," has placed these enormities in a striking point of light,

and, with his wonted acuteness of discernment, has presented, in the way of Bishop Watson, difficulties which no Christian bishop will ever be able to surmount. Murder and theft are crimes of so detestable a nature, and so destructive to the best interests of society, that they never can be sanctioned either by human or divine power. God and Moses, in these books, are said to have sanctioned both; it follows, therefore, that God and Moses are both bad characters, or else the books are not true. The latter, however, is the fact, and the character of the real God of Nature remains unimpeachable.

The character of Mahomet is of a savage, military, and tyrannical cast; but he speaks in the name of heaven, and, like Moses, pretends, that his murders, cruelties, and assassinations have been sanctioned by the divinity which he adores. He frequently begins his chapters in the name of the most merciful God; but, in the course of the chapter, is sure to consign to damnation those who do not accede to the system of revelation which he has received from God. "The chosen people of the Most High," under the Jewish dispensation, took the liberty of exercising a principle of indiscriminate extirpation toward all heathen nations; the Mahometans pursued a similar course in the destructive wars wherever they have been engaged, and to which they have been conducted by their fanatic leaders. The Christian world is not a whit behind either of these two grand divisions in the exercise of a censorious and military spirit. The crusades and the domestic quarrels of the Christian church will furnish an abundant verification of this remark.

The character of Jesus, considered in an individual and personal point of view, is of a less frightful and destructive nature.

The first and the last of these three religious impostors were ferocious men. It was necessary, therefore, to present them conjointly, reserving the character and conduct of Jesus a matter of distinct inquiry. It will not be necessary, however, to say much upon this part of the subject; for while it is admitted that Jesus, in a public and national point of view, has produced less misery than either Moses, or Mahomet, yet it is believed that the New Testament presents us with immoral deviations from principle in the personal conduct of him whom the Christian world has declared to be the only begotten son of God.

The followers of Jesus, however, have made up for his personal deficiency, and the Christian world has not been deficient in the number of fanatic phlebotomists disposed to destroy the moral and political plethora of the human race. Christians and Deists have sometimes coincided in their opinion that Jesus was a good character. This opinion, so far as it was acceded to by some of the first unbelievers, was either the result of ignorance, or an effect of fear. The Christian exalted this same Jesus into the character of a God, and, by their doctrines, made him equal to the Creator; such a circumstance struck terror into the human mind, and the idea of associating crimes with the divinity prevented independent inquiry.

The New Testament, so far as proof of this kind goes, furnishes us with facts and circumstances which make strongly against the moral character of Jesus. Beside the general duplicity which characterizes his answers to the multitude, he is guilty also of sending his disciples secretly to take and carry away a colt which did not belong either to him or his disciples. The doing of such an act in modern times would be denominated theft, even by pious Christians themselves. He is guilty of sowing the seeds of domestic and national warfare, and declaring that no man could be his disciple without hating his father and his mother; and also that he came not to send peace but a sword. If any man at the present day were to enter society with actions and avowed intentions of this kind, he would be considered as an enemy to moral virtue, and deserving of that punishment which domestic justice and public tranquility required. It is in vain to applaud the conduct and opinions of Jesus, when the same conduct and opinions applied to another being would be considered as criminal, and hostile to the best interests of human existence.

In the first edition of this work, and in the chapter concerning the immoralities of the scriptures, ideas and arguments were advanced that supersede the necessity of prosecuting farther the present subject. Moses, Mahomet, and Jesus, can lay as little claim to moral merit, or to the character of the benefactors of mankind, as any three men that ever lived upon the face of the earth. They were all of them impostors; two of them notorious murderers in practice, and the other a murderer in principle; and their existence united has, perhaps, cost the human race more blood, and produced more substantial misery, than all the other fanatics of the world.

CHAPTER XXII

Prejudices

The discovery and the development of truth, as it really exists in the system of nature, is of the highest importance to the true interests of mankind; but how to present this truth to the view of the mind in a manner calculated to attract its attention, is difficult to say; for although the uncorrupted faculties of man cannot be opposed to the attractive charms of truth, or the brilliant beauties of her native appearance, yet so numerous are the causes, and so powerful their operation which serve to mislead the mind and produce injurious impressions upon it, that perspicuity and regularity of thought are essentially deranged, and the clearness of scientific deductions are swallowed up in the gulf of error and deception. This process, prejudicial to our mental operations, commences in the early stages of our existence, and proceeds with a regularity of mischievous consequences, to the period when man assumes the dignity of intellectual independence; and fortunate indeed is that individual who arrives to this elevated predicament of mental existence. The energy of thought when applied to the discovery of truth, is naturally calculated to sweep away the rubbish of error, and cut up those deep-rooted prejudices which have so long retarded the useful improvement of our species. The grand object of philosophic philanthropists should be, to extend the sphere of mental energy, to enlarge the circle of its influence, and to oppose a persevering activity of mind to the fallen rancour of superstition, and the destroying fury of fanaticism. Religious enthusiasm, bigotry, and superstition, conjoined with the strong arm of political despotism, have rendered man in the past ages of the world the degraded instrument of their own pernicious and destructive purposes; it is here we must seek for the source of any human misfortunes, and the perpetuation of those prejudices by which the body and mind are both enslaved; it is true that the natural imbecility and imperfection of our faculties, and the extensive nature and variety of those moral and physical combinations, from which science is to be deduced, evince the strong probability that man may frequently be erroneous in the conclusions which he draws from certain premises, because the force of his faculties is not adequate to a full and complete investigation of the compounded and diversified relations of existence; but these natural obstacles to the clear deductions of science, are neither of a discouraging or an insurmountable nature.

The energy of the human mind is prodigious in the disclosure of natural principles, and its activity must be measured on a scale of endless progression. Nature is correct and righteous in all her operations; man is wrong only when he deviates from her laws. Our errors, our prejudices, and our vices, are so many instances of a departure from the beneficial laws of moral and physical existence, and our education is calculated to favor this unfortunate dereliction. The idle and foolish stories of nurses, and the still more ruinous tales and doctrines of priests, are calculated only to corrupt the heart, and bury the human mind in the gulf of the most destructive prejudices. How is it possible that man should have any clear conceptions of natural truth, when his understanding is constantly insulted with a thousand incongruous and non-existent relations, such as ghosts, witches, and devils, which perpetually disturb the imagination, and draw the rational faculties into the vortex of fancy and fanaticism? and this will ever be the case so long as superstition, or, which is the same thing, a religion claiming a supernatural birth, shall spread its bloody and baneful influence among intelligent beings. The faculties of man ought to be circumscribed only by that extensive circle which embraces the full extent of their native and accumulated activity. When religious prejudices are permitted to mingle their gloomy effects with the exalted conceptions of enlightened reason, the important cause of truth and the dearest interests of humanity become perceptibly retrograde, and darkness instead of light pervades the moral world. When Moses, by authority pretendedly divine, diffused light over the world previous to the creation of the sun, Superstition greedily swallowed the holy absurdity; but when Galileo asserted the sphericity of the earth, they cried heresy, and armed against science and philosophy, and yet the latter was an important truth in the system of nature; the former, a stupid blunder of ignorance and fanaticism. Such, O Superstition! are thy pious efforts to blind the human mind, the better to subjugate its powers, and rob man of the fruits of his industry.

There is no system either of education, politics, or religion, which ought to be excepted from the severest scrutiny of the human mind, or the closest examination which the human faculties can bestow upon it; yet habit and custom of long duration have so strongly attached man to his errors, that he reluctantly relinquishes those tenets which serve only to disturb his peace, and destroy his happiness; while the privileged impostors of the world, or those who feast upon the continuation or error and prejudice, unite their strongest exertions to persuade man that his most important interests in time and eternity depend upon the preservation of ancient and unnatural establishments; which, in fact, are as destructive to human felicity, as they are derogatory to the divine purity of supreme intelligence. The influence of authority, the fear of incurring clerical displeasure, and the dread of eternal torments, have partially annihilated the energy of intellectual powers, and taught man tremblingly to submit to the grossest imposition.

If the disclosure of my thoughts and reflections resulting from a constant habit of contemplating Nature in her diversified relations and real modes of existence, can throw a single ray of light into the darkened intellect of man, it will increase my hopes of future progression, and essentially tranquillize the sensations of my heart. It ought to be perceived by every enlightened mind, that long- established prejudices are not to be suddenly eradicated; but by protruding the activity of intellect into the field of actual existence, some diminution of human misery may be reasonably expected. Man sees not with clearness, that his sufferings are frequently the consequences of his blind attachment to error and superstition; he seeks for their origin in the distant heavens, or the anger or resentment of supposed supernatural agents, while the truth often is, that his own prepossessions are the causes of his calamity.

Nothing is more difficult, while the mind is under the influence of prejudice, than to persuade it of the necessity of removing or destroying that prejudice; prejudice destroys the discerning power of the understanding, and conviction becomes impossible while the force of evidence necessary to produce it is not discovered. The same idea of right, the same ideas of truth, associate themselves with a prejudiced mind, as are to be found in the clearest operation of the most enlightened; and the fool is as confident in error, as the wise man standing on the broad basis of moral and natural truth. No hopes of reform can be entertained relative to such obstinate minds, until you can render them susceptible of the impressions of doubt or uncertainty; the man who never doubts, or calls in question the truth of any deduction which he has made, is but badly calculated for the development of real principle; there is no extension or perfection of mind which excludes the possibility of error, and it is only by repeated examination of our own opinions, that we can arrive through the process of investigation to that elevated situation which unfolds the sublime truths contained in the system of nature.

If it were possible to conceive of a mind whose strength and energy had elevated it above all the impressions of associated life, and the deductions drawn from early combinations, and the primary influence of scientific pursuits, we should then behold the intellect of man exhibited in that point of view, which would promise a fair discussion of all the diversified relations of existence, by which we are enabled to deduce all those fundamental laws contained in the physical, mental, and moral world. But in those cases where the human mind attempts the discussion of any philosophic subject, under the impression of a previous bias, every part and view of the subject is subjected to the influence of associated habits, and the unreasonable attachment of an unrestrained imagination, or a cruel and atrocious fanaticism. This is remarkably verified by the conduct of every religious sectary in the world, whose opinions, however variant from the standard of truth, are ever considered by the individual advocate as the only true means of obtaining divine favor. The Jew, the Christian, the Mahometan, are all equally tenacious of those doctrines and opinions in which they have been educated; they contend with equal tenacity for the supposed truth of their respective tenets, and the liberal bestowment of the most virulent anathemas constitutes a prominent characteristic of each religion.

The tenacity of prejudice and irritability of temper, are not difficult to be accounted for. Every fanatic sect of religion speaks in the name of heaven. It has enlisted Jehovah on its side, it keeps up a familiar intercourse with celestial powers, and discerns, in all the operations of those powers, the most decided partiality in favor of the particular doctrines which its members have embraced. With weak and fanatic minds, the confidence is prodigious which results from a supposed alliance with heaven. A being armed in the name of a ferocious God, slaughters with relentless cruelty every other being who does not pay homage to the barbarous divinity, which his own heated imagination has depicted. No prejudices are so deep rooted, none so violent, as those of a religious nature, and their pernicious effects are generally in proportion to the ignorance of the human mind, and the barbarous condition of society. It is the light of science alone that can destroy such causes of human wretchedness; science opposes its own strength to the injurious effects of error and prejudice, and in proportion as the former shall increase, the latter will decrease; so that the hopes of the human race rest upon the diffusion of knowledge, and the general cultivation of science. Ignorance is a soil in which the rankest prejudices appear the most flourishing, and promise the greatest portion of misery to mankind. It is ignorance and interest united, which preserve the prejudices in favor of those systems of religion so injurious to the operation of intellectual power, and so destructive to the general felicity of man.

It is to be remarked, that the prejudices existing between different nations or individuals, are frequently destroyed by an extension of acquaintance, and the farther knowledge of those facts, from which righteous conclusions can be drawn; the same may be said in regard to systems, subjects, or principles. A partial or imperfect view leads to wrong attachments or erroneous deductions; while a comprehensive examination may teach the mind to suspend, alter, or rectify, its final determinations. The different religious sectaries all reject each other's doctrines, and too frequently hate and detest each other on account of difference in opinions; while the scientific mind, rising above early prejudices, perceives the errors of all parties, and pities the ignorance, which binds man to such stupid and senseless doctrines. But it is more lamentable, that such ignorance and error of mind should be found united with the grossest perversion of moral principle; a difference of opinion is followed by a most rancorous spirit of malevolence, and the exercise of the most glaring and destructive vices. It is to be presumed, however, that there is in nature a substantial foundation for moral principle; that the source of this principle is to be sought for in the organic construction of human existence; that doubts or differences upon this subject will be, in a high degree, removed, when stripped of theological delusion, and that the human mind is capable of being inspired with a moral confidence, which will seldom be shaken by the current of events, or the difficulty of new cases.

CHAPTER XXIII

Moral Principle

In the sacred writings of the Jews and Christians, in all ancient and theological compositions, the idea of correct and moral principle had been so frequently abandoned, and so grossly violated, that the energy of thought, for many ages, was inadequate to an upright and full investigation of the nature of human actions. This subject is, no doubt, connected with considerable difficulties; but these difficulties have been essentially augmented by the rubbish with which superstition has covered the moral character of man. The proofs of any inquiry, which relate to moral principle, adhere so closely to the realities of physical and intellectual existence, that the errors of an upright and intelligent mind can never assume a frightful and destructive character. They will be continually modified, and undergo frequent corrections by the new information of which the mind is continually susceptible.

Moral science cannot, perhaps, be reduced to absolute certitude, or become susceptible of absolute perfection; it is in its nature progressive, and the infinite diversity of sensations, which constitute the essential basis of all our intellectual combinations and deductions, will furnish, at least, a suspicion, that the decisions of the mind upon this subject ought frequently to be re- examined and subjected to a new and more accurate scrutiny. All the theological systems that ever have been written, have never thrown a particle of light upon this most interesting inquiry; they have established precepts, some few of which are good, and others extremely immoral; but no analysis of the physical or moral powers of man has ever been exhibited; no development of the principle of causation, or the nature of those effects, which have essentially resulted from the constitution of animal or intellectual existence. In all these cases, supernatural theology has prudently observed an absolute silence, probably from a consciousness of the most profound ignorance. This single truth, of itself, evinces the moral deficiency of supernatural religion, and the necessity of returning to the basis of nature for a correct development of principle. Every thing that is discordant to this has been established by the force of authority, and the reasonableness of such establishment has never been a ground of serious inquiry.

If it should be objected, that it is impossible, even upon the basis of nature, to find a universal standard of morality, it will nevertheless appear, that a continual approach toward such a standard must be far preferable to those arbitrary decisions which theology has made upon this subject. There can be no internal force or excellence connected with a system established solely by external power, without reference to the essence or character of the principles which constitute the body of such a system. The internal excellence of the principle itself, together with capacity of mental discernment, is essential to the ultimate benefit which may be expected from the natural operation of legal codes. But there is no better method of rendering a principle intelligible than by showing that it is consistent with nature, that it has resulted from her laws, that it is useful in its effect, that it is capable of being reduced to practice; in a word, that it is suited to the powers, condition, and character of the human species.

There is another previous consideration also, which ought to be taken into the account before we shall be able to comprehend the essence of moral principle, or to understand the nature of those duties which result from our original constitutions. That intellectual part of man, which supernatural theology has denominated a soul, has been viewed separate and distinct from the body, as a kind of spiritual and celestial inhabitant of a mean and material tenement; that their union would be of short duration, and that their final destination was extremely different. This led to reasonings and conjectures that were erroneous; for as the corporeal sensations were entirely excluded from a participation in the cause, by which moral influence was produced, an accurate knowledge of the sources of action was necessarily excluded, and spiritual mystery was substituted for philosophic demonstration.

The human mind is incapable of forming any conception of that which is not material; man is a being whose composition is purely physical, and moral properties or intellect are the necessary results of organic construction. To ascertain, therefore, the foundation of moral principle, it is necessary to revert to the physical constitution of human nature, it is necessary to go to the source of sensation, to the cause of impressions, and the diversity of these impressions; to the universality of the

fact, that all human nature possesses the same or similar sensations, together with all the other additional circumstances
resulting from the subsequent intellectual combinations of
our existence. All human beings are susceptible of pain, they
are also all susceptible of pleasure; they are all possessed of the
same senses, subjected to the same wants, exhibit the same
desires, and are satisfied with the same enjoyments. These
positions cannot be controverted, they are true in the general
features of their character, and the inconsiderable deviations
resulting from the variations of animal structure, cannot, in
any eminent degree, shake the rectitude or universality of
these positions. The modification of the principle of animal
structure in intelligent existence, is, no doubt, diversified by
a nice and inscrutable gradation, but the aggregate amount of
organic results must be nearly the same, and though the animal sensation were to vary in a still higher degree, yet it would,
nevertheless, be substantially true, that certain comprehensive
axioms might be laid down, which would necessarily include
within the sphere of their imperious effect, every possible
diversification of the sensitive faculties of human nature.

That happiness is to be preferred to misery, pleasure to
pain, virtue to vice, truth to falsehood, science to ignorance,
order to confusion, universal good to universal evil, are positions which no rational being can possibly controvert. They
are positions to which mankind, in all ages and countries,
must yield assent. They are positions, the truth of which is
never denied, the essence of which is never controverted; it
is the form and application only which has been the cause of
social contention, and not the reality or excellence of the axioms themselves.

That universality of the principle of sensation generates universal capacity of enjoying pleasure and suffering pain; this circumstance modifies the character of human actions, and renders it necessary that every man should regard every other man with an eye of strict justice, with a tender and delicate sensibility, with a constant reference to the preservation of his feelings, and the extension of his happiness; in a word, that the exercise of eternal justice should be constantly reciprocated by all the individuals of the same species. If I assume to myself the pretended right of injuring the sensations, the moral sentiments, or general happiness of my neighbour, he has, undoubtedly, an equal right to commit the same violence upon me; this would go to the destruction of all right, to the total subversion of all justice; it would reduce society instantly to a state of warfare, and introduce the reign of terror and of misery.

It is a contradiction in terms to assert that any man has a right to do wrong; the exercise of such a pretended right is the absolute destruction of all right, and the first human being who commits violence, has already prepared for himself a hell of retaliation, the justice of which his own mind can never deny. It is, therefore, inconsistent with truth to say, that there is no such thing as a general standard of moral principle; this standard has a real existence in the construction of our nature; it is ascertained and regulated by the rule of reciprocal justice. It is absolute in the most important duties of human life; but in other cases of less weight and magnitude, it is discovered by the calculations of judgment, by the process of the understanding, and will sometimes vibrate between the impressions of sense and the subtle combinations which constitute an ultimate moral decision.

If it be objected upon the suggestion of this idea, that the system of natural morality is less perfect than that which has been revealed, the true answer is, that revealed authority, in the most intelligible cases, is incorrect and absurd; and in the more refined cases of difficulty, a total ignorance is manifested; so that it is evident, upon the very face of the record, that the subject of moral principle, in its subtle discriminations, was never examined or understood by theological writers. The boasted maxim of the Christian religion, "All things whatsoever ye would that men should do to you, do ye even so to them," is incorrect in point of phraseology, and in point of principle does not exceed any of the moral writers of antiquity, who lived many hundred years before Jesus Christ. If this scriptural declaration means to establish the doctrine of reciprocal justice, it is incontrovertibly right; but the idea of placing the essence of virtue in the "wishes" of the human heart, is not very correct. It is very possible that one human being may desire another to do unto him many things which ought not to be done, and which are, in their own nature, improper or immoral. To say, therefore, that our desires should constitute the basis of moral decision, is a declaration not consistent with truth, and which, in many cases, would subvert the very essence of moral principle.

There is a fitness or suitableness in the thing itself, united with the consideration of the good or bad effect that would be produced, which ought to become the ground of uniform and universal judgment in the human mind. My neighbor may wish me to do unto him an act of serious and substantial injury, which being performed, ought to be returned to me in manner and form exactly the same; and thus, by an adherence to this maxim as it is now stated, a double injury would be produced, and the foundation of virtue shaken to the center. But waiving any criticism of this kind, and giving to this scripture declaration the full extent of what is contended for, it is, nevertheless, no more than a plain maxim of justice, which had been know and practiced, in a greater or less degree, at all times and in all countries. All the local and unjust institutions of mankind in former ages have not destroyed the essential relation which man bears to man, nor have they been able wholly to efface a knowledge of those duties which result from these relations, and from the powers and principles of human existence.

The more the subject of moral principle is examined, the more it will appear that there are certain general features in it which the experience of man has partially recognized, and being fully developed and reduced to practice, would constitute a solid foundation for human felicity. The approach to such a standard of perfection will be gradual and slow, but it must, nevertheless, from the very nature of man, be constant and certain. "The following," says Volney, "is conceived to be the primordial basis and physical origin of all justice and right; whatever be the active power, the moving cause that directs the universe, this power having given to all men the same organs, the same sensations, and the same wants, has thereby declared, that it has also given them the same rights to the use of its benefits, and that in the order of nature all men are equal. Secondly, inasmuch as this power has given to every man the ability of preserving and maintaining his own existence, it clearly follows, that all men are constituted independent of each other, that they are created free, that no man can be subject, and no man sovereign, but that all men are the unlimited proprietors of their own persons. Equality, therefore, and liberty, are two essential attributes of man, two laws of the Divinity, not less essential and immutable than the physical properties of inanimate nature. Again, from the principle that every man is the unlimited master of his own person, it follows that one inseparable condition in every contract and engagement is the free and voluntary consent of all the persons therein bound; further, because every individual is equal to every other individual, it follows that the balance of receipts and payments in political society ought to be rigorously in equilibrium with each other; so that from the idea of equality, immediately flows that other idea, equity and justice."

Again, the same author observes, that "there existed in the order of the universe, and in the physical constitution of man, eternal and immutable laws, which waited only his observance to render him happy. O men of different climes! look to the heavens that give you light, to the earth that nourishes you; since they present to you all the same gifts; since the power that directs their motion has bestowed on you the same life, the same organs, the same wants, has it not also given you the same right to the use of its benefits? Has it not hereby declared you to be all equal and free? What mortal then shall dare refuse to his fellow-creature that which is granted him by Nature? O nations, let us banish all tyranny and discord! Let us form one society, one vast family; and since mankind are all constituted alike, let there henceforth exist but one law, that of nature; one code, that of reason; one throne, that of justice; one altar, that of union."

The foregoing impressive sentiments of this celebrated writer disclose with clearness to the view of the human mind, the nature of moral principle and the foundation of all right and of all virtue. It is the reciprocation of sensation, the mutuality of condition, of powers and wants, that constitute the immortal basis of justice, and lead to the establishment of rules, whose operation must ever be in strict coincidence with the happiness of the human species. The exceptions to those fundamental principles are so few, and so unimportant, as to form no strong objection against the general assertion, that there exist in the constitution of human nature those essential properties which confer upon man the character of moral agent. To controvert, therefore, the existence of these moral principles, or the idea of a general standard in the morality of human actions, is to fly in the face of all experience, to oppose the universal consciousness of the human understanding, and deny the most conspicuous facts connected with the life of man.

CHAPTER XXIV

Matter and Power; Origin of Motion; Liberty and Necessity

The universe is composed of an infinite mass of matter; or at least, to the human mind, it is infinite, because to this mass no assignable boundary can be affixed. Space is unlimited or infinite, and in this vast expanse, innumerable bodies of matter, of different magnitudes, are continually performing variegated revolutions. Upon these bodies or higher spheres of existence, other smaller bodies are discovered, of specific modification and powers, essentially connected in their natures with the larger orbs to which they respectively belong. In all these bodies, great and small, motion is an essential and inherent property. The inactivity of matter is a doctrine contradicted by the evidence of our senses, and the clear deductions of a sound philosophy. It is impossible to conceive matter without power, or of power without matter; they are essentially connected; their existence is interwoven, and cannot be separated even in thought. The ancient doctrine of matter and motion, so long exploded, and so much calumniated by theological priests, will probably, at some future day, be considered as bearing a very strong relation to a pure and incorruptible philosophy. Supernatural religion has blinded the human understanding, and prevented upon this subject every clear and correct conception.[1]

---

[1] The New York Reviewers, in the review which they took of the first edition of this work, after quoting a number of detached sentences from this chapter, make the following observation: "Those who have read the most celebrated atheistical writers, will see that, Mr. Palmer is as determined an Atheist as any of them. "It is presumed that these learned Reviewers mean to take the Bible and Testament descriptions of God as the standard of theism. Let us then examine the case upon this ground, and we shall soon discover what it is to be an Atheist in the estimation of the New York Reviewers. "And the Lord spake unto Moses, face to face, as a man speaketh unto his friend," (See Exodus chap. xxxiii. 11). "And I will take away mine hand, and thou shalt see my back parts; but my face shall not be seen." (See Exodus chap. xxxiii. 23.) From these passages it appears, that God is represented in the form and shape of a man, and that such were the ideas of the inspired and chosen people of God concerning the Creator. But there is another passage in the New Testament, which places this matter in a still stronger light. In Paul's Epistle to the Hebrews, speaking of Jesus Christ, he says that he was the brightness of his father's glory, and the express image of his person. Now both believers and infidels agree, that Jesus was in the shape and form of a man; and as he was like God, of course God must be like him; therefore, the Christian God is like a man, perhaps like one of the New York Reviewers. Now the fair deduction from all this is, that whosoever doth not believe that God is like a New York Reviewer, is a most profane and abominable Atheist. What a sublime and majestic spectacle of theism do these "learned" men present to the human mind! In another place they charge the author of this work with "affectation, inordinate vanity, and the want of comprehensive views." How wonderfully comprehensive must be the views of those who can place the material universe upon the shoulders of a God, resembling in his existence a New York Reviewer. Such "literary" heroes ought triumphantly to exclaim, that they have excelled in brilliancy of conception, and in comprehensive views, the story of the Indian, which places the earth upon a turtle's back, and then declares the turtle stands upon nothing! Permit "us" miserable Atheists to bow with great humility before such "splendid" talents, and such "comprehensive views." Go on, gentlemen Reviewers, and console yourselves in the preservation of that Trinitarian or polytheistical scheme of religion to which you are so much attached; but remember, the moment will arrive in the succession of future ages, when those very mental "energies" of the intelligent world, which you sneer at so much,

A belief in spirits had nearly, at one time, overturned the empire of real existence; the power and excellence of matter were exploded to make room for a world of fictions; of phantoms and things that had in nature no positive, no real, or substantial being. Filled with this idea, the dreams of theology were substituted for philosophic truth, and fanaticism usurped the domination of reason. Philosophers joined in the race of spiritual or material glory, and the united effect of their different opinions constituted the annihilation of nature. The spiritualists contended against the matter, and the materialists against spirits; thus sweeping away, by their opposite systems, every species of existence. Matter, and its diversified modes of operation, are the only things of which human intelligence can take cognizance. It is this vast body of which demands our most serious investigation; it is this in which we are interested, and with which we are most closely connected. Much has been said concerning dead or inactive matter; much concerning its "vis inertia"; but an appeal may be safely made to the phenomena of the physical world for a complete refutation of this opinion. Every fact that strikes our eyes, or presents itself to the contemplation of the understanding; every movement in nature furnishes argument against a doctrine so unphilosophic and erroneous. Every thing that we behold; all the elements are in continual flux; agitation or motion is a universal and eternal law of nature. The earth, the ocean, and the atmosphere, are constantly in a high degree of action; the evidence of these facts are presented to every living creature. The raging

---

will sweep away the whole bundle of theological nonsense, leaving only the mighty power by which the universe is sustained; and of the shape or form of this power, the New York Reviewers have as little idea as "the author of the Principles of Nature," or any of the profane and abominable Atheists, whom the advocates of Christianity long ago sent down to the dismal abodes of the damned, to dwell for ever in hell fire.

element of fire is never wholly at rest; it is always powerfully or more silently operating in every part of the world. If these ideas are controverted, let man inquire into their truth by an immediate recourse to the energetic movements of physical existence. In regard to fluids, this opinion, perhaps, will not be controverted; but it will be asked, whether it be equally true in regard to solids? To this, the answer is unequivocally in the affirmative; at least so far as it relates to the question, motion or not motion, action or not action. Beside the general revolutionary motion which the earth has round the sun, the parts of its solid materials are constantly combining and dissolving, as may be proved by the smallest recurrence to the organic structure of vegetable and animal life, and the property of disorganization essential to each specific mode of existence. It will, however, be contended, that if this be true in regard to organic matter, or to vegetable and animal existence, it will not hold equally in regard to other portions of the material world. There is, undoubtedly, a difference in the activity of matter, or in degrees of motion, of which the several parts are capable; but there is no such thing as absolute incapacity of motion; no such thing as absolute and entire rest. For the truth of this, an appeal is made to the power, pressure, and dissolving operation of the most inert and stupid portions of material substance. An appeal is made also to the activity of the most stupid parts of matter, in the composition of vegetable productions. What regular industry do the solids and fluids exhibit in the formation of a common vegetable? The march of each particle to its destined post is with firm and philosophic step; with constancy and physical zeal. There is no such thing as dead matter; all is alive, all is active and energetic. The rays of the sun fructify the earth, and these are considered among the portions of dead matter. These rays, however, are so active, as to travel 95,000,000 of miles in the space of seven minutes and a half; a celerity of motion which substantiates, beyond all contradiction, their essential power and activity. Every fact, in the physical world, forces conviction in the human mind, and proves the energetic nature of the material system. An investigation of the properties of matter, a full development of its modes of operation, would lead to the most salutary consequences, by instructing man in regard to his true predicament in nature, and reconciling him to his fate. To corroborate the ideas which have already been suggested upon this subject, the following strong and philosophic reflections are taken from an anonymous pamphlet, entitled, An Essay on Matter. "All matter is possessed of life, spirit, action, or motion. What is called inanimate matter, owes its motion of life no more to the elements, than what is acknowledged to be animate. This elementary influence presupposes the animation of bodies; for as these cannot move without that influence, so neither can that influence where there is no life. To say that the elements alone give motion, is to say that the elements give life, which is denying a universal agent, or making him appear to act more by intermediate agents than philosophy will allow. No one, I presume, will doubt the independent motion of matter in that form which we name animal, at least, that it is as independent as man; we allow animals to be a composition of matter without soul, yet we allow them to be possessed of the principle of motion. It is from this motion solely that we allow them to be possessed of life; for there is nothing beside that can or does influence the mind to make it assent to this truth, that animals have life; and it is from the different combinations of motion and matter that we form our ideas of the different kinds of animals. It is then from motion, and nothing else, that we judge of, and allow matter of a particular kind of composition to be possessed of the living principle; the same evidence must have the same weight in every other kind of composition. Wherever motion is discoverable in matter, be the form of it what it may, we must acknowledge it to entertain the living principle; but it may be said, that though motion be an evidence of life in matter in certain forms, and where the motion is of certain kinds, yet motion of every kind will not prove the existence of life in matter of every form. This absurdity of supposing a 'caput mortuum', must appear to every one who considers the connection and dependence which exits in all bodies upon each other, the motion which this connection supposes, and life which motion evidences. There is a perpetual exchange of matter with matter of every form. The animal creation, for instance, is constantly exchanging parts with the earth and its atmosphere. If the matter composing animals be animate, and that of the earth inanimate, how can these be united? This would be to suppose that two opposites could exist in one body, whereas it is the nature of opposites to recede from each other, and nothing can be greater opposites than life and death. The independent motion of matter in that form called vegetable, can be as little doubted as in animals. Storms, earthquakes, fires, floods, do not cause vegetation any more than they do generation in animal. The natural or preternatural motion of bodies, no more contributes to the motion of matter in vegetables, than in animals; they, like us, receive only the natural and gentle influence of the elements, and thereby mark a link in that chain which connects all matter, and which is the harmony of creation. We shall be more particular in speaking of motion in vegetables, when we come to treat of the nicer operation of matter in that action which we call thinking. We come now to speak of the motion of matter in those forms where it is less observable upon a superficial view of things; but where, upon a nearer view, it is not less evident than in either of the other forms mentioned.

"Whoever doubts the motion of matter in the form of a stone, let him take the trouble to look upon the first rock in his way, and he will see its surface mouldering. Whatever decays, must be replenished; for matter cannot waste. Stones, then, give to, and receive matter from other bodies. Circulation is a very perfect motion. Will any one assert, that the motion of giving and receiving of its substance, does not exist in the stone, with only that assistance, which, in common with us and animals, it receives from the elements? The motion of matter in the various forms of minerals is more observable, as it is more lively. There is a constant fluctuation of matter in all mineral bodies. When miners open a mine, and do not find the ore they are in pursuit of, in the quantity which they expected, they say the mine is not ripe, and close it up again, that the metal may have time to grow. If matter have not the vital principle, then I have the power of creating. The bulk of my form is increased by the matter which in the action of eating, inspiration, and absorption, I add to myself. If this matter have not the principle of life, how can I make it partake of me, and thereby partake of life? Can I unite dead and living things, or can they be united in me? Chemists tell us that the union of bodies depends upon the affinity, i.e. the likeness which matter in one form has to matter in another form, and tell us no further. We have before mentioned the different kinds of union produced by affinity, the perfect and imperfect; but what gives the quality of union, and preserves the existence of the compound? It is the living principle in one body, inclining it to associate with the living principle in another body. Without this living principle, that inclination which supposes motion could not exist."

The above observations exhibit, with philosophic clearness, the nature and property of matter. It is by a constant recurrence to the operations of the material world, that man will be able to discover those solemn and important truths on which his happiness is founded. Our bodies are composed of the elements, compounded and organized by the skill and energy of nature; from this organization, certain consequences necessarily result; composition, decomposition, and recomposition, are established in the order, and supported by the laws of physical existence. The materials which are employed in any specific composition possess inherent and indestructible qualities, but the result may be augmented and power increased by organic construction. Thus, for instance, matter in its most simple form, may, perhaps, be destitute of intelligence; but when combined and modified in the form of a man, intellect is a uniform consequence. It is impossible to say, how far the properties or qualities of matter may extend in a simple and uncompounded state. It is impossible from the want of communication, to affirm, or deny with absolute certitude, relative to the internal essence of the particles of material existence. There must be in the essence of matter a capacity, when combined in certain forms, to produce specific results. The principle of life must be essentially inherent in the whole system and every particle thereof; but to attribute to each particle a specific kind of life analogous to that which is discovered in large compositions of matter, cannot, perhaps, be warranted by the knowledge or experience of nature. In all the specific modifications of life, disorganization, or death, is a universal law; but the universality of this law among specific combinations upon the earth, cannot, perhaps, be extended to the earth itself. The analogy is broken, when we go from individuals or particulars to generals or universals. But more of this hereafter.

It is by the laws of motion that combinations are formed, it is by the same laws they are dissolved. Motion is an essential property of universal existence. The following paragraph upon this subject, is taken from the System of Nature, a powerful work, translated from the French of the celebrated and philosophic Mirabaud.

"Every thing in the universe is in motion; the essence of nature is to act, and if we consider attentively its parts, we shall see that there is not a particle that enjoys absolute repose. Those which appear to us to be deprived of motion, are, in fact, only in relative or apparent rest; they experience such an imperceptible motion, and so little marked, that we cannot perceive the changes they undergo. All that appears to us to be at rest, does not remain, however, one instant in the same state. All beings are continually breeding, increasing, decreasing, or dispersing, with more or less dulness or rapidity. The insect called 'Ephemeron' is produced and perishes the same day; of consequence, it very rapidly experiences the considerable changes of its being. The combinations formed by the most solid bodies, and which appear to enjoy the most perfect repose, are decomposed, are dissolved in the course of time. The hardest stones are by degrees destroyed by the contact of air. A mass of iron, which time has gnawed into rust, must have been in motion from the moment of its formation in the bowels of the earth, until the instant that we see it in this state of dissolution." Mirabaud's System of Nature, Vol. I. page 42.

A philosophic investigation into the laws of nature, would probably furnish a pretty clear solution of all the phenomena of the intellectual world. A certain portion of matter organized upon a certain specific plan, produces, in the animal we denominate man, all the energetic and astonishing effects of mind.

A question has been stated among speculative meta-physicians, whether it be not probable that the earth and all the higher spheres of existence in the planetary world, are possessed of strong intellectual powers? Indeed, this conjecture has been carried so far as to combine the whole of material existence, and attribute to it all the properties, qualities, and powers of intelligent life. Nature is considered as possessing a central power, a brain, or cognitive faculty, whose operations on a higher scale are supposed to be analogous to the brain or thinking faculty of man. And this, perhaps, would be the most philosophic method by which to arrive at the idea of supreme intelligence, or the governing power of the universe. But whether the planets in their individual capacity be considered as intellectual beings, or whether nature in its aggregate combination be thus considered, are questions of speculation, concerning which, perhaps the human mind will never receive any adequate or satisfactory information. Man, however, should not fear to extend his contemplation to the whole of nature, and, if possible, subject the whole to the powerful examination of his intellectual energies.

From the ideas that have been disclosed in this chapter, it will be easy to perceive, that if the inquiry were now made, "where is the origin of motion?" the philosophic answer would be, that it is in matter itself, co-essential and co-eternal with it, and cannot be separated from any part thereof, not even in thought.

A further question, in some measure connected with the present subject, is that which relates to the principle of action in the mind of man, or the opinions relative to Liberty and Necessity. Moralists and meta-physicians have for a long time been in a state of altercation on this subject, nor is the point of discussion between them yet completely settled. Perhaps the preceding reflections may furnish us with some information and aid in the solution of a problem so difficult. The principle of motion and action must exist essentially somewhere; if this principle be in matter itself, or in a foreign agent whose existence is presumed to be wholly extraneous from the body of nature, the same consequence will, however, necessarily follow. Man is an organized being, possessing powers of motion and action; if the motion of which man is susceptible be the result of the essential nature of matter in specific organic construction, the motion in this being must be as independent, absolute, and self-existent, as in the body or any part of nature; that is, it must belong to the thing itself, co-essential with its being, and acting by the internal force of the principle itself. If the principle of motion be sought for in any intellectual agent foreign to the body of nature, it must be independent and absolute there; it must be self-existent, and as man must have proceeded from one or the other of these two sources, he must be like the source itself from which he emanated, and possess, in a partial degree at least, that independence of power and action, which are so justly to be attributed to these two great sources of all existence. To suppose an infinite series in the principle of causation, exhibits nothing more than a feeble effort of the mind, to get clear of a metaphysical difficulty. The last point that is discovered, includes in it an equal necessity of discovering another point, on which the last may depend for its existence. The links in this chain would become innumerable, its length infinite, and, after all, the difficulty remain as great as ever.

This doctrine, concerning the origin of motion, and of giving a solution to the subject by means of an infinite series in the principle of causation, can never satisfy the mind that is seriously in quest of a first point, or essential spring of every action; in short, it is nothing better than the story of the Indian, who placed the earth upon a turtle's back, and afterwards declared, that the turtle stood upon nothing. The fact is, man is independent in his mind; it is the essence of his nature to act, and he feels, or ought to feel, that he is not the slave of any of the phantoms of superstition, or the fine spun reasonings of metaphysical philosophers.

In a moral point of view, the doctrine of necessity is still more objectionable, and goes to the destruction of all human merit, and with it the dignity of the human character. If man be a moral slave, his actions in relation to himself are neither good nor bad; he is impelled by an irresistible necessity, and can no more in justice be punished for his conduct, than a cannonball, which is propelled forward by the explosion of gunpowder, can be punished for taking off a man's leg. The one upon the doctrine of necessity is as much a moral agent as the other, and punishment, in both cases, equally absurd. It is essential to the dignity of man that he be free and independent, both morally and politically. Political slavery is not more derogatory to the human character, and human energy, than moral slavery. They both sink and brutalize mankind;

they both have a tendency to diminish his efforts, and destroy his active zeal in the cause of virtue. It is essential to the true and elevated character of an intellectual agent, that he realize the strength of his powers; "that he be confident in his energies;" that he hold in suitable contempt every species of moral and political despotism. This sentiment will raise him from a degraded condition, and form him into the stature of a perfect man in the glorious system of nature.

CHAPTER XXV

Commencement of the Nineteenth Century; Christianity; Deism; Reason; Science; Virtue; Happiness

The nineteenth century opens to the human race with prospects of a most extraordinary and astonishing nature. It is impossible, at this moment, for the human mind to contemplate the past, and anticipate the future, without yielding to the mingled emotions of regret and joy; without perceiving itself to be alternately agitated with sentiments of misery and happiness. The commencement of a new century necessarily revives the idea of a recursive view of those great events which have had the most powerful influence, and produced the most important changes in the condition of human society. The history of mankind has, in general, consisted either of uninteresting details, or a frightful picture of universal carnage and military ferocity. During the last century, however, something more valuable and important has been combined with a mass of historic matter, and amidst the unjust and destructive wars which the poison of monarchy is still generating in the very bosom of the community, there is to be seen a splendid display of those philosophic principles which sustained the universe, and of those moral axioms which are essentially interwoven with intelligent life, and by which it is rendered susceptible of universal amelioration; of those political laws whose essence is at war with tyranny, and whose final effects will shake to the centre the thrones of the earth.

It has been during the last century that these things have been accomplished; the force of intellectual powers has been applied to the development of principle, and the combination of human labors already constitutes a colossus, against which the storms of unequal and aristocratic governments may dash in vain. The art of printing is so universally known, or rather the knowledge of it is diffused in so many countries, that it will henceforth be impossible to destroy it. The present moment exhibits the most astonishing effects of this powerful invention in the hands of nations, by that universal diffusion of principle and collision of thought, which are the most substantial guarantee of the future scientific progress of the human race. An effectual stand has been made, and resuscitated nations at this moment bid defiance to the double despotism of church and state.

The nineteenth century opens with lessons awfully impressive upon kings and tyrants; with lessons, the truth of which has already penetrated into the sacred recesses of ecclesiastical wickedness and spiritual domination in high places. America, France, Switzerland, Italy, Holland, Germany, and England, are in a high state of intellectual fermentation; if the government in some of these countries acts in opposition to the spirit of improvement, this circumstance will constitute only a partial drawback on the rapidity of the progress; the general agitation is national, the power of thought has become vastly impulsive in all these countries. The printing-press is operating, and if it be in some measure restrained, it will, nevertheless, gradually undermine, and eventually subvert the thrones of civil despots, and teach the hierarchy of every country, that the time is fast approaching in which, if they pretend to speak in the name of Heaven, they must exhibit unequivocal proofs of their celestial authority; it is this pretended intercourse with Heaven that has subverted every thing rational upon earth. Upon this subject, and in describing the fatal effects of fanaticism, the following passage from an original and eccentric writer ought to be quoted. The passage exhibits in strong colors the indiscriminate folly and mad enthusiasm of which ignorant and uninstructed man is susceptible.

"It has been the constant practice for moral doctors or teachers to pretend to a new faculty of mind, called inspiration, or communication with supernatural power; this is practiced by priests in all parts of the world, from the Lapland Magi to the civilized Pope, and if it was not an insult to good sense, to attempt, with argument, the refutation of such absurdity, I would observe, that inspiration, in proportion as it approaches and identifies with Deity, the common source, the diversity of its streams or opinion is augmented; the inspired Catholic abhors the inspired Protestant, this the inspired Jew, the Jew the inspired Mahometan, and when these bedlamites break loose, their victims burn each other at opposite piles, despising that inspiration in others which they rage with themselves.

"I know but one remedy for this moral pestilence of superstition, which is, to assemble the inspired idiots of all countries, that the view of their contortions, convulsions, and delirious ravings, in the presence of each other, might exhibit the portraiture of folly in so strong a light, that Reason would burst her sides with laughter, and Judgment must be restored." "Revelation of Nature."

The meek and humble character of Christianity in its origin, the fanatic zeal of its partizans, and the pretended renunciation of worldly grandeur, led to a conclusion, that every attempt of uniting with political tyranny would be pointedly discarded by the votaries of this new and supernatural religion. The subsequent history of the Church has, however, placed an indelible stamp of error upon this opinion, and proved that the intimate associates of the celestial Jesus were willing also to become the associates of terrestrial lords, for the purposes of acquiring the support and strength of tyrannical governments. Those who declared that their kingdom was not of this world, were soon discovered to be willing to unite with the kings of the earth, justly considering that earth and heaven united would be competent to every object, even the universal subjection and slavery of the human race. Such was, in a high degree, the effect, when Christianity was embraced by the strong arm of the Roman government. This holy religion at first sought for simple protection from the mistress of the world: but no sooner was this accomplished, than a new and more impulsive desire was perceived to be the ruling sentiment of the Church, and it claimed from the civil power toleration in all religious and ecclesiastical concerns. This new success was followed with a new exhibition of ambitious views, and the open disclosure of a bolder confidence in the ultimate triumph of the then infant church of Christ. Spiritual domination, and the ruling of nations with absolute despotism, which at first constituted no part of the feeble hopes of

Christian believers, was at length attempted, and the success of the attempt was completely satisfactory to the most ardent hopes of the new hierarchy.

Thus it was that the meek, the humble, and the poverty-struck followers of the meek and humble Jesus were transformed into what sectarian secession has since denominated, "the scarlet whore seated upon the throne of the Caesars." This event was followed by many centuries of Christian barbarism, in which the spirit and principle of the Gospel triumphed over and subverted every species of science, and buried beneath its despotic weight the intellectual energies of the intelligent world. This long period has been justly denominated the night of ignorance, and may, with equal propriety, be denominated the pure and uncontaminated reign of the Christian religion; because it was at the period that the authority of the church was complete, and the civil power was subjected to its absolute will; because at that time the ecclesiastical dominion was believed to be essentially incorporated with the purest directions of the founder of that holy religion; and because every subsequent secession has, in the estimation of the mother Church, been considered as a damnable heresy, and an awful departure from the true faith.

These secessions from the original Church have constituted a cause which has been gradually operating for the amelioration of the human species, and which must ultimately terminate in the triumph of reason over the compound despotism of the world. The Church of Christ received its death wound by the conduct of two bold and fanatic leaders of the two grand sectaries which first protested against the unqualified authority of the Roman Catholic Church. Luther, and

Calvin, with more fervent zeal and holy piety than those whom they opposed, nevertheless, laid the foundation of sub-sequent events, calculated to overturn every species of ecclesiastical dominion, and bury in one common grave the various branches of celestial tyranny, which for many ages had held the world in bondage.

The spirit of sectarianism spread itself far and wide, dividing and diversifying the opinions of the Church, and each new sectary seemed to be endowed with a new portion of that rancorous malignity, which has so universally marked the conduct of those whose pride and folly have led them to conclude, that they spoke in the name of heaven, and were the favorites of the Most High. Such sectarian altercations, however, were destined eventually to destroy each other. Men of contemplative minds began at length to suspect the divine originality of a religion, which branched itself into so many different species of doctrines, and generated amongst its professors endless wars.

Another consideration still more powerful, accelerated the progress of moral improvement, and constantly diminished the force of attachment toward the Christian system. Every new sect discarded some of the absurdities of that from which it had separated, and passed a general sentiment of condemnation upon all those who were in the rear of this long and religious train. Luther and Calvin hurled their religious thunderbolts against the power and absurd tenets of the Church of Rome, and especially against the Pope, by whom this Church was governed. The Armenians, the Arians, the Socinians, and the Universalists, successively followed, with a purifying hand of reason, pruning and lopping off the decayed branches of the old theological tree, approaching still nearer to the source and principles of nature, till at length, by regular progression, the human mind discovered, that moral principle was placed upon a more solid foundation than the reveries of sectarian fanaticism. It has been in this manner that some portion of society has once more obtained a true idea of the religion of nature, or of that which may be denominated pure and simple Deism.

It is this religion which, at the present period of the world, creates, such frightful apprehensions in the household of faith, and threatens to shake to the center the chief corner stone on which the Church is built. These apprehensions are daily disclosed by Christian professors, and they depict in such strong colors the fatal effects of Deism, that ignorant fanaticism believes it to be an immoral monster, stalking with gigantic strides over the whole civilized world, for the detestable purpose of producing universal disorder, and subverting all the sound principles of social and intelligent existence. Such are the horrid ideas which the enemies of this pure and holy religion are every where propagating amongst their credulous and deluded followers. This circumstance renders it necessary, that the true idea of Deism be fairly stated, that it may be clearly understood by those whose minds have hitherto been darkened by the mysteries of faith.

Deism declares to intelligent man the existence of one perfect God, Creator and Preserver of the Universe; that the laws by which he governs the world are like himself immutable, and, of course, that violations of these laws, or miraculous interference in the movements of nature, must be necessarily excluded from the grand system of universal existence; that the Creator is justly entitled to the adoration of every intellectual agent throughout the regions of infinite space; and that he alone is entitled to it, having no co- partners who have a right to share with him the homage of the intelligent world. Deism also declares, that the practice of a pure, natural, and uncorrupted virtue, is the essential duty, and constitutes the highest dignity of man; that the powers of man are competent to all the great purposes of human existence; that science, virtue, and happiness, are the great objects which ought to awake the mental energies, and draw forth the moral affections of the human race.

These are some of the outlines of pure Deism, which Christian superstition so dreadfully abhors, and whose votaries she would willingly consign to endless torture. But it is built upon a substantial foundation, and will triumphantly diffuse happiness among the nations of the earth, for ages after Christian superstition and fanaticism have ceased to spread desolation and carnage through the fair creation of God.

In surveying the history of man, it is clearly discovered, that the miseries and misfortunes of his existence are, in a high degree, the result of his ignorance and his vices. Ignorance renders him savage and ferocious; while science pours into his mind the benign sentiments of humanity, and gives a new coloring to his moral existence. Reason, which every kind of supernatural theology abhors; reason, which is the glory of our nature, is destined eventually, in the progress of future ages, to overturn the empire of superstition, and erect upon its ruins a fabric, against which the storms of despotism may beat in vain, against which superstition may reek her vengeance without effect, from which she will be obliged to retire in agonizing tortures.

It has been the opinion of some honest and intelligent minds, that the power of intellect is inadequate to the moral and political emancipation of man. This opinion, though sometimes it is found to be operative upon benevolent hearts, seems, however, to be at war with the intellectual structure of our existence, and the facts furnished by modern history. In the great question which relates to human improvement, the cause which is productive of thought, cannot, in any high degree, be included as influencing the final decision. It is probable, however, that the opinion which refers intellect to organic material combination would favor most an unlimited improvement of the human species. If thought be an effect of matter finely organized, and delicately constructed, the best method of augmenting its power would be, to preserve the whole human system in the most pure, regular, and natural mode of operation. Parents and instructors, in this respect, are capable of doing great injury, or of producing most important benefits to future ages.

The science of the world has been, in some measure, diminished by the propagation of an opinion, that there are only a few human beings who are possessed of what is called genius, to the exclusion of all the rest. This looks too much like mystery, and seems to include in it the idea that man is sent from heaven, to occupy for a short time a miserable and material tenement, and then return to its native home. It ought to be recollected that earth is the abode of man, and that of this the materials of his existence are composed, all are confined to this place of residence, and to the amelioration of sensitive and intelligent life all his labors ought to be directed. He should learn to respect, and not despise his reason. He should learn to consider moral virtue as the greatest good, as the most

substantial joy of his existence. In order, however, to be emi-
nently good, a full scope must be given to the operation of
intellectual powers, and man must feel an unqualified confidence in his own energies.

The double despotism of Church and state has borne so
hard upon human existence, that man is sunk beneath its
dreadful weight. But resuscitated nations are about to teach
kings and tyrants a lesson awfully impressive, in regard to the
destiny that awaits the aggregate injustice of the world. The
period is at hand, in which kings and thrones, and priests and
hierarchies, and the long catalog of mischiefs that they have
produced, shall be swept away from the face of the earth, and
buried in the grave of everlasting destruction. Then will the era
of human felicity, in which the heart of unfortunate man shall
be consoled; then will appear the moment of national consolation, and universal freedom; then the empire of reason, of science, and of virtue, will extend over the whole earth, and man,
emancipated from the barbarous despotism of antiquity, will
assume to himself his true predicament in nature, and become
a standing evidence of the divinity of thought and the unlimited power of human reason.

CHAPTER XXVI

Philosophical Immortality

"See matter next, with various life endued, Press to one center still, the general good. See dying vegetables life sustain, See life dissolving vegetate again: All forms that perish other forms supply, By turns we catch the vital breath and die. Like bubbles on the sea of matter borne, They rise, they break, and to that sea return."

— Pope's Essay On Man

The subject of a future life, has, in every age and country, in a greater or lesser degree, engaged the attention of man. That strong sentiment by which we are attached to life, has given to human sensations a most powerful impulse, and induced us to overleap the boundaries of the visible world, and seek in unknown or non-existent countries, the continuation of that existence which experience taught us it was necessary to abandon here.

The diversity of opinion that has prevailed upon this subject shows the difficulties which in some measure are essentially connected with the nature of the inquiry. The strong and active impulse that binds man to his personal identity has led to extravagant conceptions concerning the means of his preservation, and the new modes of existence, which, in the succession of ages, he imagined hew was destined to experience. Religious fanaticism has indulged itself in the most unguarded manner, and enlisted heaven, earth, and hell, on its side, the better to accomplish its purposes; while philosophy, disgusted with the wild vagaries which religious imposture every where presented, seemed to incline to the opposite extreme. A contest commenced which has not yet terminated, and which presented alternately to the hopes and fears of man, the means of satisfying the one, and of destroying the other. Real consolation, however, was not furnished to the human mind by the virulence of their diversified discussions. It was to be expected in a case embarrassed with so many difficulties, that speculations would be endless, and decisions extremely variant.

As it commonly happens that people see more ghosts and spectres in the dark than in the light; so in the present case, the eagle eye of Superstition saw, or pretended to see, in the distant ages of futurity, and in the strange countries to which every intelligent being was hastening, all the peculiarities and local circumstances which would hereafter encircle the life of man. Thrones were erected, marble seats prepared, pomp and splendor in abundance, as the portion of that select company, whose ardent and fanatic hopes gave them a full assurance of a triumphant entry into the mansions of eternal glory; while, on the other hand, the hot, sulfurous, and infernal abodes, presented to the vicious and panic-struck mortal the dreadful considerations which stand connected with the idea of endless torture. Philosophy viewed the frantic ravings of religious enthusiasm with a mixed sentiment, composed of compassion and disgust. She sought in the constitution of nature for the discovery of some solid truths on which intelligent man might repose his existence, without fear and without trembling.

The progress of thought upon this subject has excited in superstitious minds the most rancorous sentiments of malignity; opprobrious epithets have been let out in abundance, merely because Reason labored to discover, and declared that it had in some measure discovered, the real connection between man and nature. The terrific idea of annihilation still hovered around the dreaming abodes of Fanaticism, and the most substantial and philosophic truth, which a knowledge of nature presented to man, became the ground of a most personal persecution and envenomed malice. Theology, however, frequently exhibits her weakness by condemning in others what might with great justice be charged to her own account.

If we advert for a moment to the sacred writings of the Jews and Christians, the folly of their high pretensions to a superior immortality will become very visible. The Old Testament furnishes no information relative to the subject of a future life. "Dust thou art, and unto dust thou shalt return: man has no preeminence above a beast, as the one dieth so dieth the other," are phrases contained in the Old Testament; and are sweeping clauses against every hope of a future life, so far as such hope is founded upon this part of revealed religion; but it will be said, that the Gospel has brought life and immortality to light, and on this account rises in its claims to respect above the contemptible materialism of modern philosophy. It is true that the New Testament speaks of a future life; of Heaven and Hell; of the resurrection of the dead, &c. but it is necessary first to prove the truth of this part of the system before substantial deductions can be drawn in favor of any species of immortality. It is very easy to make naked and unsupported assertions, but unless the reason and evidence of the thing accompany these assertions, they are good for nothing. Paul, speaking of the human body, and of the resurrection of the dead, says, "It is sown a natural body, and it is raised a spiritual body;" by what kind of chemical process it is that matter is to become spirit, must be left to Paul and other spiritual chemists to determine.

The physical universe presents to the human understanding a grand and important spectacle of contemplation, in which the whole and the parts are essentially and indestructibly connected. There is no such thing as flying off in a spiritual or metaphysical tangent; every thing is bound by eternal laws to pass through the routine of its successive modes of existence, through the processive changes to which the laws of matter and motion have destined it.

There are two species of philosophical immortality; first, the immortality of matter, in its essential nature and character; and, secondly, the immortality of sensation in the aggregate mass of sensitive and intelligent life. These two perceptions must form the basis of every thing comprehensible upon this subject. The first needs no particular explanation, as the truth of the axiom, "that something can never become nothing," is now generally admitted to be true; but the second idea ought to be rendered more intelligible. The opinions upon this subject have always supposed the existence of a spiritual, immaterial, and indestructible soul, which was capable of making its escape through the body, and passing in a light and airy manner through the atmospherically regions, spending an unconfined and uncontrollable existence in a manner inconceivable by our gross senses in their present condition.

The doctrine of transmigration is a branch of this system, and supposes that the souls of men may pass into other animals of an inferior kind, and reside there for a given time, by way of atonement for past crimes. These ideas of intellectual transmission, of solitary and distinct spirituality, are among those theological departures from philosophic truth which reason has to deplore, and which have retarded, in a very considerable degree, the progress of knowledge. It is in vain for man to deceive himself; a knowledge of his true condition in nature, and his relationship with all existence, will furnish a consolation far superior to all the theological reveries of antiquity. Matter is every where in motion; it is matter and motion, or the laws of the material world, by which innumerable sensitive and intelligent creatures are successively modified and disorganized. The rotation is eternal, and all the parts of nature may in time pass through the strictures of animal existence, and partake of the capacity of enjoying pleasure or suffering pain. In this warfare there is no discharge; an undying succession, an immortal mutation awaits the existence of every living creature. Nothing is durable in regard to modification or identity. In short, nothing is immortal but matter, its combinations and results; to wit, sensation and intellect.

But it is easy to perceive, that the continuation is specific and not personal; that man is destined to pass through an infinite diversity of predicaments, partaking at all times of the immortality essential to matter, and the perpetuated immortality of sensation in successive forms of animal existence.

That this idea, so far from terrifying his mind, should furnish it with instructive lessons of sympathy, justice, and universal benevolence.

If it should be objected here, that this is not the immortality to which man is so strongly attached, the answer is obvious, he must be reconciled to that kind of immortality, which nature prepares for her children, and which diffuses through the intelligent world a sentiment of equality, terrifying to every species of spiritual or political aristocracy. It has frequently been said, that the ardent wishes of the human mind, in regard to immortal existence, furnish strong presumptive proof in favor of retrospect identity; but this error is visible upon the very face of the record. Thousands of individuals most ardently wish to continue their life here for ever; but this furnishes no barrier against the certain approach of death and final dissolution of the body. Human nature is accustomed to wish for more than it can obtain; its wishes, therefore, can never be brought as the standard of truth. It might as well be expected that man should become immensely rich, because he wished to be so, as that he should immortalize his personal existence by the extent of his desires in this respect. It is true, however, that whatever does exist must continue to exist for ever; this assertion regards substance and not forms; forms continually perish, but the essence of things is indestructible.

The ancient and orthodox idea is, that the (1)universe, with all its component parts, was made out of nothing; and if so, it must remain nothing, for it must be of the essence of which it was composed. It is a gross error to imagine that the eternal nature of things can be changed or destroyed by the operation of any power whatever. The great machinery of nature is governed by immutable laws; its motions are the result of its own internal energy. Hence it may be inferred, that it is at once the cause and effect; the mode and the substance, the design and the execution, and active and never ceasing operator. [1. Some of the remarks herein contained are taken from the manuscript of a philosophic friend.]

The existence of man is essentially connected with this vast whole, and it is impossible that he should ever detach any part of himself from the immortal system of which he forms a component part. The intervolutions of matter with matter, are universal and eternal; the essence of which man is composed, will therefore eternize its reciprocal relation with the vast fabric of material substance, which is presented to intelligent beings throughout the regions of space. A comprehensive view of the energies and relations of the material world, would, no doubt, shake to the center the theological absurdities of antiquity; but it would leave to contemplative man the high consolation of having discovered from what source he originated, and to what destination the unalterable laws of nature have devoted his existence.

The highest intellectual joy consists in the discovery of truth; a knowledge of this truth will constantly tend to the practice of an exalted virtue; this virtue will serve as the stable foundation of human happiness, the immortal guarantee of the felicity of the intelligent world. Reason anticipates a progress, which all the powers of superstition can never arrest. Let reason then perform her faithful duty, and ignorance, fanaticism, and misery, will be banished from the earth. A new age, the true millennium will then commence; the standard of truth and of science will then be erected among the nations of the world, and man, the unlimited proprietor of his own person, may applaud himself in the result of his energies, contemplate with indescribable satisfaction the universal improvement and happiness of the human race.

THE END